THE MANTLE:
How to
Dress for Success
in Leadership

THE MANTLE:
How to Dress for Success in Leadership

All Bible references taken from the New King James Version unless otherwise noted.

First Printing by Cornerstone Publishing, Inc., P.O. Box 2896, Virginia Beach, Virginia 23450.

Second Printing by Mantle Ministries, Inc., PO Box 248, Lanoka Harbor, NJ 08734

Cover and cartoon illustrations: Robert A. Thomas, Cover design: Gann Graphics, Editing: Susan Bohannan and Nicole A. Hartis

Library of Congress Cataloging-in-Publication Data

Biscardi, James, 1942 –
The mantle: how to dress for success in leadership / James Biscardi, Jr. p. cm.
    ISBN 1-882185-42-0 (pbk.) 13-digit ISBN 978–18821854–2-9
    1. Management—Religious aspects—Christianity. 2. Leadership-Religious aspects— Christianity. 3. Jesus Christ—Leadership.
I. Title.
HD38.B565 1996   96-21190
658.4'09 - dc20   CIP

First printing, 1996   Revised Edition printing, 2009

Printed in the United States of America

THE MANTLE: How to Dress for Success in Leadership

James Biscardi, Jr.

TABLE OF CONTENTS

INTRODUCTION

Billy Graham said that the wonder of Christ's resurrection and the message, "Jesus is alive!" lifted Christianity out of the category of dead superstitions and archaic religions.

The angel's declaration, "He is not here; He is risen!" changed the course of history, brought hope to a hopeless world, and gave believers a purpose and a power they had never known.

God became man to dwell among us and to die on the cross for us. Because of that death and atonement, all who accept Him can be saved. Jesus Christ has given believers great hope and assurance for eternity. Eye has not seen, nor ear heard, nor has it entered into the heart of man, what God has in store for us!

As a result of His victorious resurrection, our Good Shepherd has empowered us to live proactively that abundant life which He demonstrated before us. In addition, He gave His Word as a legacy of solutions to our world's most perplexing problems. Above all, He established a right relationship with our Heavenly Father and showed us how to love and serve Him and each other. He also demonstrated an inspiring leadership style that transcends earth's pilgrimage in time. Christ's leadership style is the subject of **The Mantle: How to Dress for Success in Leadership.**

The New Testament tells us that God has vested in Jesus Christ all power in heaven and on earth, and He is seated at the right hand of God, the Father. One day, He will return with His saints to rule the world and will make us both kings and priests. We will simultaneously rule with Him as "kings" and serve humanity with Him as "priests."

Jesus and His leadership principles are the same yesterday, today and forever. What He demonstrated as leadership during His short visit with us will be the world's standard when He returns. His leadership behaviors are suited for when our borders are expanding or when they require downsizing. They are applicable to leaders in the four major enterprises of life: **The Workplace, The Church, The Home, and The School.** Men and women who practice Christ's leadership style experience a purpose and power to transform lives and enterprises that they never knew was possible.

The Mantle is written to help workplace leaders, husbands, wives, parents, pastors, other church leaders, and educators visualize Jesus in their vital leadership roles. It is written with the hope of energizing leaders' cooperation with the Lord in revitalizing the four enterprises most crucial to life on the planet. Each of these — **The Workplace, The Church, The Home, and The School** — seems to be in the quicksand of history:

The Workplace. "Every year since 1988, at least one-third (and sometimes more than one-half) of large and midsize companies have reduced their work forces, according to surveys of the American Management Association (AMA). More often than not, one round of downsizing merely leads to another. Two-thirds of corporations that thin their ranks one year follow up with another purge the next, reports AMA. These repeat restructurers, rather than becoming lean and mean, often end up lean and lame . . . and send some of their best workers (the ones they would most like to keep) scrambling for the exit. Eighty percent of downsizers admit that the morale of their remaining employees has been mugged." This is what was reported in the January 10, 1994 issue of *Fortune Magazine* in an article titled "Getting Beyond Downsizing." It has continued to be true.

Was it necessary to downsize? Was the creativity of front-line employees explored to improve the business' "bottom-line" before the decision was made? And what about the survivors of these purges? How should they be managed? Let's remember that these sullen, dispirited, burdened-down folks are the very people who are supposed to revitalize our enterprises and delight our customers. These "walking wounded," the broken pieces of downsizing and other management practices, can't reenergize our organizations if they fear their number will come up next. Says Robert Tomasko, author of the book, *Rethinking the Corporation*: "You've got a lot of shell-shocked survivors, and now you're forcing them into task forces to reengineer how work is done. Come on, there's tremendous unreality to that."

On March 22, 2009, the New York Times reported, "Though job losses accelerated last month, the United States has not yet hit bottom…the Labor Department said that almost 600,000 jobs disappeared in January 2009 and that a total of 3.6 million jobs had been lost since the beginning of the recession in December 2007. The unemployment rate , meanwhile, rose to 7.6%…Losing more than a half million jobs in each of the last three months, the country is trapped in a vortex of plunging consumer demand, rising joblessness and a deepening crisis in the banking system…the contraction of jobs is already steeper than in any recession since at least the early 1980s."

The Church. Undoubtedly, workplaces need to adopt a better leadership model — especially during downsizing, but, lest we forget, the Church has discouraged and disillusioned shell-shocked people as well. It wasn't too long ago that there seemed to be an outbreak in our churches of men and women in "trusted" positions who abused or broke that trust. Large ministries, grossing millions of dollars every year, supporting programs in many parts of the world, were torn apart by their leaders' mismanagement, corrupt, unethical practices or immoral behavior. It was left to the management staffs to put back together and try to restore and build back up the broken "people" pieces left in the trail of such leadership philosophies. These are only the public abuses. How many more "walking wounded" people in churches suffer in silence under dictatorial, abusive or just uninspiring church leaders? Leaders need to consider seriously why 20 percent of church members do 80 percent of the work. Perhaps we need to be reminded of Jesus' leadership style that inspired men and women to sacrifice their very lives.

The Home. Even the most essential building block of our country's unity, the family, has suffered miserably because of separation and divorce. The spouses and children who need to be managed back to "health" by a stepfather, stepmother or new spouse have become "survivors." The family needs to be restored — along with the unity, mutual love and respect among its members. New family "leaders" need to deal with their spouses' and children's hurts and disappointments and with the "broken" trust.

The School. In many public schools we have children being removed by parents, who have begun creating "charter schools." These are schools run by parents, in cooperation with each other, to educate their children. These "charter school" children join the long line of "private school" and "home school" children, many of whom have become the survivors of the public system. They, as well as those remaining in the public system, are the "educational disabled" who need to be nurtured back to health by educators who follow Jesus' leadership behaviors. In many of our elementary and secondary schools as well as in our colleges and universities, students have been scarred by uninspiring, immoral and abusive practices by their teachers and athletic coaches.

As these profit and non-profit enterprises consider how to become more efficient or how to revitalize themselves, they need to consider adopting a model for leaders that will restore the trust that's been broken and build up people while (if necessary) they build down the organization. At the same time, the model needs to develop in the work force (the associates of the enterprise) a heart to continue providing good customer service. Profit and non-profit organizations as well as families are looking for answers: How do we manage our people to "do more with less" or to "work through the adversity"? How do we involve them in the process of continuously improving the enterprise? For those who have been downsized (workplaces or families), how do we manage the shell-shocked survivors and get them to go beyond themselves to produce, when they have lost fellow workers or have been separated or divorced? For those entrusted with the "educational disabled," how do we heal the scars, restore their self-esteem, and make them society's major contributors again?

What's needed is NOT SOMETHING NEW. People and the essence of their lives — their needs, desires, hungers and hurts — are unchanging. What's needed is to adopt a regular diet of the right *people*-management habits. It's learning to do the right things right the first time when it comes to managing people. What's needed is a leadership model that develops caring managers, throughout the enterprise, who involve people in developing a vision for continuous improvement and renewed growth. Managers need to accept, recognize and reward contributions. They need to build a trust that empowers people to be creative decision-makers and makes "teamwork" a way of life. What's needed is to use the benchmark left to us by the Master Builder and Manager, Jesus Christ.

He managed a small group of 12 disciples who efficiently and effectively turned the world upside down, promoting substantial changes in religious doctrine. He has sustained for 20 centuries His ideas and solutions to life's uncertainty and tribulations. He has managed and energized millions of disciples. How did it happen? How does it continue? What are the behaviors of management that Jesus has demonstrated to us? Using Christ's biblical teachings has been highly successful for me. *The Mantle* represents over 35 years of personal experience as a church leader and a workplace supervisor managing small groups as well as a multi-service organization of 150 employees with 24 subordinate managers. Even when one considers numerous management practice success stories in industry for producing high quality products and services, the similarity to Christ's behavior is remarkable.

The Christ leadership model — one which is participative, incorporating ideas such as the servant-leader who facilitates the work of "subordinates" rather than directing or "bossing" them — still works miracles to transform enterprises into progressive organizations with motivated people who want to increase profits or, in general, bring about success. We call this model **MAN**agement **T**hru **LE**adership **(MANTLE)**.

A mantle in biblical days was a sleeveless cloak or loose garment worn around the shoulders, covering other garments — a symbol of authority that was passed on to one's successor. Recall the description in 2 Kings 9-13 of the prophet Elijah who was about to be called home to heaven. His disciple Elisha asked him for a double portion of his spirit. Elijah told him that only if he sees him taken to heaven could that wish be granted. So Elisha followed his master with excitement and anticipation wherever he went. Finally, God sent a fiery chariot to carry Elijah to heaven and because Elisha was faithful to see it happen, Elijah dropped his mantle for Elisha. When he put it on, Elisha indeed had the double portion of power he desired.

The use of the mantle garment by its biblical wearer gives today's leader (at the workplace, at home, at church, and at school) a good example of what he must provide for those entrusted to him. He needs to be a *covering, protector, comforter and instrument of empowerment. He must serve and provide freedom, identification and recognition for his people to help them through the uncertainty, change, broken trust and chaos they experience in the world. We leaders need to be examples of what we want our people to become, with them watching us closely, so that the "mantle" (or power) will fall on them.* Then workers will serve one another either individually or as teammates as their manager serves them.

The mantle garment attributes that do reflect Christ's leadership behaviors and promote the highest achievement in

10

others are explained in the chapters that follow. It is sincerely hoped that the reader (workplace manager, employee, pastor, deacon, teacher, spouse and parent) will find practical guidelines for improving and energizing the management-employee, pastor-deacon-church member, husband-wife, parent-child, teacher-student relationships. Often in this book workplace terminology is used to express the concepts. However, examples, personal testimonies, and MANTLE challenges for the home, the church, and the school are included so the reader can see the application for these enterprises as well. *The Mantle* is organized around the eight major leadership behaviors demonstrated by Christ:

> Be open to other people's ideas - listen
> Building up our people's self-esteem
> Being loyal and building loyalty
> Good communications and planning
> Building unity and family
> Recognizing and rewarding good performance
> Rating performance well
> Developing a "heart" for serving customers

WITH MUCH GRATITUDE . . .

I'd like to thank my pastor, Rev. Joseph DePasquale, and my good friend, Rev. Peter Lambo, for their advice and guidance in The Mantle project. I also want to acknowledge my appreciation to Rev. Guy BonGiovanni for his sincere and very helpful critique of an early draft. Many thanks also to the workplace and church friends for their suggestions, support and encouragement. As always, Patty, who is my wife, dearest friend, and partner deserves a combat ribbon for her patience and for her unshakable belief in me throughout this new adventure in writing. Most of all, my thanks and praise to our Lord Jesus Christ, who was not only the inspiration for The Mantle, but also my "behind the scenes" Servant-Leader and Motivator.

Chapter One
GOD MAKES LEADERS, THEY'RE NOT BORN

What Is The Process? How Does It Happen?

We are simultaneously both leaders and followers. At the workplace we follow our supervisor, while at church we lead a small group Bible Study or a Sunday School class. Perhaps we lead as an elder or deacon. At church, we follow a pastor, while at home we lead our family. At the workplace or in the classroom we're a team leader or teacher, while at home we're a son or daughter following our parents.

We need to recognize that every Christian believer is a leader. Jesus gave us the great commission to teach "all nations, baptizing them in the name of the Father and of the Son and of the Holy Spirit, teaching them to observe all things that I have commanded you" (Matthew 28:19,20).

As God told Elijah to anoint Elisha (1 Kings 19:16,19) to take his place, similarly, He gave Jesus direction and authority to anoint every believer. As Elijah cast his mantle upon Elisha, so Christ casts the mantle of the Holy Spirit upon every believer. Just as Elisha, who wanted a double portion of Elijah's spirit, was required to keep his eyes upon Elijah, likewise we go in the power of the Holy Spirit, and we keep our mind stayed upon our great High-Priest, Servant-Leader, who is the Lamb upon the throne. Yes, every believer is a leader; however, we are simultaneously called to follow as a minister.

This is God's way to make us into servant-leader, MANTLE

13

managers. The best training for becoming God's leader is to be faithful in serving others in our dual roles of leader and follower — to become a living sacrifice for the Lord, not conforming to the world's view that leadership is something to be wrestled away as quickly as possible, from the higher authority. We need to be transformed by Christ's example of a humble servant who became obedient unto death — the death of the cross — and let God do the "exalting" (e.g. progressively giving us more responsibility, both secular and spiritual) in His time.

MANTLE managers are developed over time by being servant followers. While we have the Holy Spirit mantle, He leads us into the desert of learning as He did Christ, Moses, Paul and other great biblical heroes who became servant-leaders. We progress through degrees of leadership responsibility while being a faithful follower. We receive the fullness of our mantle (e.g. the visible "robe of righteousness"), when, like Elisha, we've learned to serve our Elijah. Our desire to have a double portion of power is patiently set aside while God forms Christ in us. He does this by testing our faithful support (with good will, speaking the truth in love) of the Lord Himself and then the leaders — both spiritual and secular — He gives us. We are yoked together with Christ in spirit and with our leaders in earth's very practical mission endeavors.

In our dual roles, we need to ask the Holy Spirit to make us sensitive to His still, small voice as we study His Word and observe the needs, activities and especially the behaviors of those we lead or follow. *The Mantle: How to Dress for Success in Leadership* has been written to help us focus more clearly on Christ's servant-leader behaviors and to allow the Holy Spirit to strengthen us in these behavioral areas — to make more profitable our trek in the "desert of learning" to be like Christ.

What does God look for as the raw material to work Christ — the Servant Leader — into us?

"Let this mind be in you which was also in Christ Jesus, who, being in the form of God, did not consider it robbery to be

14

equal with God, but made Himself of no reputation, taking the form of a servant, and coming in the likeness of men. And being found in appearance as a man, He humbled Himself and became obedient to the point of death, even the death of the cross. Therefore God also has highly exalted Him" (Philippians 2:5-9).

The first raw material God looks for is not to be anxious to rise to leadership. God leads, and we follow. His plan for our lives is to prosper us and to give us an "expected" end (Jeremiah 29:11). The word *expected* in Hebrew means "a hoped for end." We need not be anxious. His timing is always "in time" — not behind and not ahead of time. We can trust our Father as Jesus did. We simply follow Jesus as did Simon of Cyrene, who bore His cross and followed Him to Calvary.

Even further than *not* being anxious about leadership, God wants us *not* to seek any reputation. Though He wants us to have a servant's heart, even to seek a reputation of being a wonderful servant is not what He wants. All the glory goes to Christ. He makes something beautiful about our lives — not us. He does the work. Next, God looks for the raw material of being able to relate to all men. "There, but for the grace of God, go I" material. The grain of wheat (John 12:24) material that will be "ground into flour" to bring the Bread of Life to all men. He looks for the meekness (e.g. teachableness) to be directed for service at the slightest tug of the Master and the perseverance to endure hardship, while learning to have compassion on all men. And finally, He looks for the raw material of humility to trust Him and to listen. To develop us, He will need to lead us into places where we won't want to go — like Peter (John 21:18).

Will we trust in the Lord with all our hearts and lean not on our own understanding? (Proverbs 3:5). Will we believe in Him? Will we believe that "all things work together for good to those who love God to those who are called according to His purpose" (Romans 8:28)?

The Great Fisher of Men leads us often into deep waters where only Christ's outstretched, nail-driven hands provide the strength to keep serving others. We learn that it was not the nails that held Christ to the cross. Through it all, He presses into us the servant-leader qualities of self-sacrifice, faithfulness, endurance, patience and love. Look at some examples: Joshua followed Moses for 40 years before leading the Israelites into the promised land. Would he ever get his chance? Moses served as a shepherd for his father-in-law for 40 years in the desert — unaware that God was grooming him for servant leadership. Paul studied in Arabia 14 years under Christ, by revelation, before leading others on missionary journeys — and that was after studying under one of the greatest Jewish teachers, Gamaliel. Jesus served his family for 30 years, increasing in wisdom and stature, and in favor with God and men (Luke 2:52) before His public ministry started.

Listen to what Jesus says about learning to serve: "Just as the Son of Man did not come to be served, but to serve, and to give His life a ransom for many" (Matthew 20:28). "For who is greater, he who sits at the table, or he who serves? Is it not he who sits at the table? But I am among you as the One who serves" (Luke 22:27). "If I then, your Lord and Teacher, have washed your feet, you also ought to wash one another's feet. For I have given you an example, that you should do as I have done to you" (John 13:14-15). Do we ever receive MANTLE graduation certificates? When's graduation?

We are leader-pilgrims in the world wearing the mantle of the Holy Spirit. When are we the MANTLE manager, servant-leader, that the Lord wants us to be? Does God's development process ever end? The answer is that as long as the natural man lives in us, we never arrive. Though we surrender to the Lord's correction, and he (e.g. the natural man) is progressively reduced in us so that Christ might increase, while we sojourn here, we are always the Lord's leadership "trainees." While we serve others here, we are in training for a wondrous assignment He has prepared for us.

Scripture tells us that the resurrected and raptured believers are dressed in glorious white robes (e.g. mantles) in heaven. We are told that after the rapture of the Church (1 Thessalonians 4:14-17), at the Judgment Seat of Christ, we will receive crowns; also, that we will throw these at the feet of Christ (2 Corinthians 5:10, Revelation 4:10-11).

In place of these crowns we will receive a mantle of light that we will carry throughout eternity and "shine as the brightness of the firmament . . . as the stars for ever and ever" (Daniel 12:3). Elijah dropped his mantle for Elisha, but he received a glorious one from the King of kings, who is always the Lamb upon the throne.

One day we — with Elijah, Moses, Paul and all other believers — will descend with Christ to defeat the antichrist and the armies gathered at the Battle of Armageddon (Revelation 19: 11-16). We will follow the great Light of the World. We will be wearing the eternal mantle of light and be dressed in fine linen, white and clean. It will be a glorious procession from heaven to earth — the Sun of Righteousness clothed in a mantle of brilliant smaller stars that will be flowing behind Him as every eye beholds the return of Christ.

When Jesus returns, He will be the same Servant-Leader we know Him to be. We are in leadership training now because He has an assignment for us: We shall reign with Him as kings and priests (Revelation 5:10). We shall be leader-kings and simultaneously be servant-priests to the people. We will be MANTLE managers, servant-leaders, who yielded to His instruction in our simultaneous, dual roles of leader and follower at the workplace, the home, the school, and the church.

Managers need to be a showpiece for employees

Chapter Two
QUALITIES OF THE MANTLE MANAGER

The Servant-Leader

As the mantle "served" its biblical wearer, so also workplace managers, pastors and church leaders, teachers, parents and spouses should perceive themselves as servant-leaders to those entrusted to them.

While spending time with His disciples one day, Jesus spoke to them and to the multitude around Him, "He who is greatest among you shall be your servant" (Matthew 23:11). On the occasion of celebrating the Passover, before the crucifixion, He laid aside His garments, took a towel, and girded Himself. The tradition was that a servant would be available to wash all the Passover guests' feet, but there was no servant, and His disciples were arguing about which of them would be the greatest. They were too "big" to do such a demeaning task. Jesus poured water into a basin, began washing the disciples' feet, and wiped them with the towel which was around Him. When He finished, He said, "You call me Teacher and Lord, and you say well, for so I am. If I then, your Lord and Teacher, have washed your feet, you also ought to wash one another's feet. For I have given you an example, that you should do as I have done. . . . If you know these things, happy are you if you do them" (John 13:13-17).

On another occasion, Jesus said, "Whoever desires to be first among you, let him be your slave — just as the Son of Man (referring to Himself) did not come to be served, but to serve, and to give His life a ransom for many" (Matthew 20:27-28). This is where the concept of a Servant-Leader originated.

In traditional organizations, the chief executive officer (CEO) is considered the most important person, for whom everyone else works. He's the head, and the employees are the feet. He's the highest, and the front line employee is the least. Other managers fall somewhere in between. In more enlightened organizations, that "pyramid" thinking is being turned upside down. The front line workers that "touch" the customers are considered the most important — and everyone else, including the CEO, only facilitate the front line, so that they become empowered with authority and abilities to satisfy the customer. Truly the "greatest" in today's organizations — ones that are managed to get maximum quality — are the servants of most of the people. They are "washing the feet" of the front line with quality training, open and honest communication, company values, and empowerment to make decisions at the lowest possible level.

The Home And The Church

In some families, husbands mistakenly lord it over their wives, confusing headship with dictatorship. F. Carter Smith, in his article, "I Would Have Killed Her" (*Newsweek Magazine*, July 4, 1994), writes:

> I got married when I was 19. My wife, Janet, was 18. At the time, I was a student pastor for the United Methodist Church up in east Texas. The first time I became violent with her we had gone to a meeting, and I thought she was creating a public display. So once I got her alone, I slapped her to get her to quiet down, and she did. For many years after, she was living in fear of the next time. I was following what I thought the Bible said about what a family should be, that the man

should be the head of the house and be in control. That led me to directing what she did and where she went. We went on without physical violence, but I was shouting, balling up my fists and letting her know I was certainly willing to use violence.

In Ephesians 5:25, however, the Apostle Paul says, "Husbands, love your wives, just as Christ also loved the church and gave Himself for it."

Husbands need to "turn the pyramid upside down" and become the servant-leader that Jesus has become to the Church. Some pastors and other leaders behave toward other members of the church in a way that some husbands behave toward their wives — allowing their positions of authority, their educational advantage, and their biblical role to become a means for "putting down" other people and keeping them in a position of servitude. These must also turn the pyramid upside down.

Heart-To-Heart

As the mantle provided warmth to the wearer, likewise leaders at all levels and in various enterprises need to give their people the "warmth" of knowing that they are their leader's highest concern and most precious asset.

Two important qualities of the servant-leader and MANTLE manager are:

>To know his workers
>To be sensitive to their needs

There's a heart-to-heart management technique today called **Management By Walking Around** (MBWA), in which a manager gets out from behind his desk on a regular basis and goes out and talks to the workers. I've used this approach and find people making comments such as, "He's a person just like us," or "I can talk to him, and he listens."

An executive at my workplace recently told me that he had

become so proficient at this that a simple handshake and asking the question, "How's it going?" let him know a great deal about the needs of the organization. Managers should get out as often as possible to really know the strengths, weaknesses, personalities, needs and aspirations of our people. That's the only way we'll know enough about our workers to take them from being "directed" to being "empowered." Needless to say, husbands, wives and children need to also make time to communicate with each other. Pastors and teachers need to get to know their congregations and students if they expect to reach inside with their message.

Jesus put it this way, "I am the good shepherd; and I know My sheep and am known by My own" (John 10:14). Speaking of the good shepherd, Jesus said, "To him the doorkeeper opens; and the sheep hear his voice; and he calls his own sheep by name and he leads them out" (John 10:3).

Man was created to fellowship with God; but that fellowship was broken when Adam and Eve sinned. God wanted that fellowship restored so he came "in the flesh," as Jesus Christ, to die in our place *and* to show us what He was really like.

Jesus said, "He who has seen Me has seen the Father" (John 14:9). He also showed us that he cared enough to suffer our temptations. The scripture says, "For we do not have a High Priest who cannot sympathize with our weaknesses, but was in all points tempted as we are, yet without sin" (Hebrews 4:15). Jesus knows what it's like to be you and me. He cares enough to have even the hairs of our heads numbered (Matthew 10:30).

The commitment Jesus wants from us is not to follow all the rules or the whole law out of obligation. That would put us in bondage to fulfill every point of the law. Instead, Jesus paid the price for our breaking the law when He died on the cross and suffered the pains of hell — since death and eternal separation from God was the penalty for breaking the law. He became human to pay our debt, and now we are free to serve Him from our hearts, motivated by love and not fear. Jesus said, "If you love Me, keep

My commandments" (from the heart) (John 14:15). "If anyone loves Me, he will keep My word" (John 14:23). In a similar way, managers, pastors, parents, spouses and teachers must understand that we are dealing with human beings with feelings, concerns and hopes for the future. We need to get a heart commitment from them to gain their full productivity potential — and we need to be sensitive to those things that will reach the heart of people. Concern for people's needs and knowing them — even to the intentions of the heart — is a cornerstone of Jesus' management philosophy.

See how the Apostle Paul learned both the principles of "servant-leader" and "heart-to-heart" as he describes his approach to bringing the message of salvation to many types of people: "For though I am free from all men, I have made myself a servant to all, that I might win the more; and to the Jews I became as a Jew, that I might win Jews; to those who are under the law, as under the law, that I might win those who are under the law; to those who are without law, as without law (not being without law toward God, but under law toward Christ), that I might win those who are without law; to the weak I became as weak, that I might win the weak. I have become all things to all men, that I might by all means save some" (1 Corinthians 9:19-22).

Wisdom From Above

The mantle provided the wearer with protection from the elements. It needed to be complete, without holes that let the rain through; and not so thin that it gave no resistance to the wind. As the wearer depended upon his mantle, a manager's people will count on his good judgment to enable them to "press on" through the storms.

Recently, I asked my Sunday School class for qualities of leadership. They came up with the following:

Expect excellence
Be compassionate with failure
Compromise

Be organized
Be honest
Keep your word
Gain respect and loyalty
Faithfulness
Discipline
Value people
Have a peaceable spirit

We then discussed what one of the greatest leaders of the Bible considered most important and found it closely compared to their list. The leader was Solomon, whose wealth, prestige and ability to influence others to build quality products was without equal. I've always been amazed how the temple was built to precise specifications, since much of the actual stone cutting took place away from the building site. For this work he used 30,000 men — 10,000 at a time — to travel to Lebanon, 70,000 men to be burden bearers, 80,000 men who were stone hewers and 3300 subordinate managers. That's a manager to employee ratio of 1 to 60, which most of our companies would envy today.

When given the choice to receive from God anything he would like, this great man asked for wisdom. Solomon considered wisdom the most important tool for a manager. The scripture says, "And God gave Solomon wisdom and exceedingly great understanding, and largeness of heart like the sand on the seashore. . . . he was wiser than all men . . . and his fame was in all the surrounding nations" (1 Kings 4: 29-31). My Sunday School class looked for a definition of this wisdom God gave him. The scripture says, "The fear of the Lord is the beginning of wisdom, and the knowledge of the Holy One is understanding" (Proverbs 9:10).

James 3:17 says, "The wisdom that is from above is first pure, then peaceable, gentle, willing to yield, full of mercy and good fruits (some translations say goodness, fairness, genuineness), without partiality and without hypocrisy."

Besides being a "servant" and establishing a "heart-to heart" relationship with workers, spouses, children, church members and students, a leader must have this wisdom that is from above. His motives must be pure. His spirit should bring peace and quiet confidence when everyone else seems to be storming. He must treat people with sensitivity to their special circumstances. He must be willing to yield to people's ideas. He must be compassionate with failure — not criticizing and threatening, but causing the person to learn from mistakes. He must gain respect and loyalty by being fair and genuine, keeping his word.

Pull – Don't Push

Let's continue using Elijah's mantle to describe one more value. A cloth garment has no "pushing power." Try to push something with a cloth garment and you'll go nowhere because it bends. The mantle, however, has "pulling power." Tie it to an object, and it will follow you wherever you go. So as Christian leaders, we shouldn't be twisting our people's arms to make them do something – or backing them into a corner or making them feel guilty or manipulating them into submission. That's not Christ. If we're to emulate Christ, then we need to learn to "wrap our mantle around others" and draw them to us – and eventually to Christ.

In Matthew 11:28 29, Jesus says, "Come to Me, all you who labor and are heavy laden, and I will give you rest. Take my yoke upon you and learn from Me, for I am gentle and lowly in heart, and you will find rest for your souls." Jesus draws us to Himself. Even when His requirements seem difficult, we do what He wants us to. For example, "If anyone desires to come after Me, let him deny himself, and take up his cross, and follow Me" (Matthew 16:24). We follow Him because He is everything we want to be – and as we follow Him, we are becoming like Him.

Pushy, dictator-type management might bring about outward compliance, but good leadership creates an inner willingness to follow because of the behavior of the leader. This is what results by using MANTLE management.

The Mantle and the Cross of Christ

As a servant leader, there's great gain - no loss.
It's the <u>self-sacrifice</u> of Your cross.[1]

Being heart-to-heart is Your shepherd's mind -
The <u>love</u> of the cross to care and be kind.[2]

Wisdom from above, You've said, is first pure.
That's the <u>holiness</u> of the cross for sure.[3]

You say, "Come unto me." - You don't push but pull.
<u>Humility and obedience</u> of Your cross, so full.[4]

Make these qualities in our lives be ample.
We humbly receive from You our Christlike mantle.

And whenever we're tempted to be a typical "boss,"
We'll faithfully remember there's no crown without Your
cross.

Our outward actions (i.e. our behaviors) always flow from
our inward values. We've been describing character qualities of
the MANTLE, Christlike, leader. They are the inward
framework around which we build our behaviors. Let's now
focus on those outward activities that come from embracing the
Servant-leader, Heart-to-Heart, Wisdom from above, and Pull-
Don't Push leadership qualities.

---

[1] John 3:16
[2] Romans 5:8
[3] 2Corinthians 5:21
[4] Philippians 2: 7-8, Matthew 16:24

Chapter Three
BE OPEN TO THE
IDEAS OF OTHERS - LISTEN

The mantle was a free-flowing garment. It allowed freedom of movement in almost any direction.

Creativity Needs To Be Biological

Who's in the best position to satisfy the customer and increase company revenue? The CEO? A financial manager? Any manager? Practically speaking, it's really those hardworking men and women who "touch" the customer day in and day out. Who can improve the process of getting a car off the assembly line with the best quality? It's the people who work in that process every day. It's the front line assembly worker who actually "touches" the car. Who can suggest best how a church can improve support to the process of evangelizing or educating young people? It's those on the "front line" in the streets or in the classrooms who've been trained and are doing the job.

These people who have ideas will improve our enterprises, but how can we tap this creativity if these people are living and working in an atmosphere of "my way or the highway" dictatorship management? How can we expect people to feel free to suggest improvements if we micro-manage them? We need an environment where creativity is expected to be part of everyone's daily routine — on the job, at church, in the home, and in the classroom.

Change and continuous improvement must become a way

of life. Creativity must become a biological part of the organization. It's not something that should only be done once a week when a quality group meets — although using this technique can be fruitful. Creativity does not begin when we enter the quality circle conference room. MANTLE managers must encourage and track ideas as an integral part of the fabric of our organizations — as important as tracking the quality of the product or service we provide.

We must convey that everyone takes part in improving the product or service and incorporate suggestion mechanisms into our daily work or home routines that reward creativity. Many mechanisms can be created, but the main ingredient in all of them is listening on the part of management. In the home, husbands need to listen better to ideas from their wives and children; and wives, who are to revere their husbands (Ephesians 5:33), need to count their spouses' ideas as real possibilities and make them feel that their ideas are important. In addition, children need to be encouraged by parents, who hold criticism to a minimum, to share from their vast storehouses of imagination.

As managers, pastors, parents, spouses and teachers, we need to learn how to foster innovation from personalities that are different from our own. Many good ideas are lost because managers say, "They don't make sense to me." Often, that's because managers are not being open and objective. We must learn to listen without the restrictions of our own preferences and experiences.

Proverbs 1:5 says, "A wise man will hear and increase learning, and a man of understanding will attain wise counsel." Proverbs 18:13 says, "He who answers a matter before he hears it, it is folly and shame to him."

So we need to give consideration to all ideas and not react negatively because we didn't think of it or because it's coming from someone who "never gets it right."

"Therefore, my beloved brethren, let every man be swift to hear, slow to speak, slow to wrath" (James 1:19).

28

The Example Of Jesus Christ

In Jesus' life we see Him accept many ways that seemed strange to others. One example was the woman who washed His feet with her tears and wiped them with her hair. This happened in the house of Simon, the Pharisee. He didn't treat Jesus very cordially at his home. He didn't kiss him warmly, which was the custom in greeting house guests — nor did he provide for the customary foot washing. This woman, repentant over her sins, fell at Jesus' feet and began washing His feet, kissing His feet, and wiping them with her hair. Simon thought within himself that if Jesus were a prophet, He would know that this woman was a sinner, and He wouldn't allow her to do these things. Jesus simply reminded Simon about the customs he had not observed and pointed out that this was fulfilling that custom (Luke 7).

In another instance, a woman poured expensive ointment over Jesus' head, and His disciples became disturbed that this perfume could have been sold and the money given to the poor. Jesus said that the poor would always be with them, but He would not. He explained that this woman had prepared Him for burial (Mark 14:3-8).

At the wedding of Cana, the groom had misjudged the amount of wine they needed for all the guests, so when Jesus' mother realized it, she asked Jesus to make some wine for them. Though He mentioned to her that "His hour had not yet come," He performed the miracle of turning water to wine. Jesus put the idea of helping the two who had just been joined in marriage before His own plans and timetable (John 2).

There's a wonderful announcement of the Lord's coming given in Isaiah 42:3. It says that "a bruised reed He (Christ) will not break, and smoking flax He will not quench."

Perhaps this scripture would best be used in the area of building self-esteem, which is described later in this book, but I believe it can also be used here to emphasize the need to encourage creativity. A "reed" was used as an instrument by the shepherds who would make holes in it to create something like a flute. After playing many tunes on it, the reed would become too soft from all the saliva and become useless. The shepherds would then throw it away. This is what is called a "bruised reed." The "smoking flax" refers to a candle that has just gone out but is still an ember. Jesus wouldn't break a bruised reed upon finding one. Instead, He would repair it somehow and play music through it again. Similarly, Jesus would not extinguish the candle that's smoking. He would fan it and bring life and light to it. That's what managers can do with people when we encourage them to make suggestions — when we show them that they are useful, creative people whose ideas are valuable to our organization.

Many people who have worked for a supervisor, pastor, teacher or parent who used criticism, threats and other management fear tactics have turned off their creative capacity. They are afraid to suggest anything or try anything new for fear of making a mistake. These people are "bruised reeds" and "smoking flaxes" that need encouragement to create once again. We ALL have good ideas. We are made in the image of God, the Creator.

The following is a testimony of former foster child, Christine Suguitan ("Healing for My Broken Heart," *Decision Magazine*, January 1994). She had to be healed from a feeling of low self-worth and uselessness. She was a "bruised reed" that the Lord renewed through foster parents. Now *she* is a foster parent, breathing new life into another wounded child. She said:

> Last year my husband and I were foster parents to a 13year-old girl who had a gloomy attitude toward life. It was as if she were voicing a silent message that said, "I'm nobody." I understood how she felt. I was able to tell her that God showed me that I am valuable to Him and that she also is valuable to God. She still telephones me often, and I know that God is using me to make a difference in her life. As I look back on my life, I see God's hand plunging through every circumstance to bring hope and love to a lost and lonely little girl. The life that God has brought to me is a

dance in the sunlight, a shout of joy. He has healed my broken heart.

THE MANTLE:
Challenges for the Church, the Home, and the School

BE OPEN TO THE IDEAS OF OTHERS - LISTEN

1. THE MANTLE CHURCH

a. Pastor has an open door policy.

b. Prayer requests are solicited using leaflets in the pews.

c. Suggestions are requested for Sunday school, children's church, Wednesday/Sunday services, and other outreaches. Speakers are often requested by church members.

d. Pastor and other leaders conduct meetings as a facilitator and coach to determine the mind of the Spirit through others, rather than dictating answers or manipulating to get preconceived answers.

e. The board of trustees (or overseeing body of the church) and the pastor work cooperatively with each other and are open to one another's ideas and opinions.

2. THE MANTLE HOME

a. Parents foster creativity in children by stimulating imagination with games, stories, videos, music, toys, drawing, etc.

b. Parents ask children what they would do in various situations. If the parent decides a different course of action, the child is told why.

c. Parents look for opportunities to do things suggested by the child.

d. Husbands and wives are open to each other's suggestions and promptings. They see themselves as equals with different roles, each having ideas that complement the other's.

3. THE MANTLE SCHOOL

a. Teachers don't just lecture. They encourage different opinions, ideas and discussion by building leading questions into their teaching plans.

b. Teachers are open to student redirection of the material being presented, as long as requirements are fulfilled.

c. Administrators encourage and listen to teachers' suggestions about the classroom activities and subject matter.

d. Teachers and administrators are open to parents' discussions concerning their recommendations and their children's special problems.

Chapter Four
BEING LOYAL & BUILDING LOYALTY

As the wearer begins to gain confidence in using the mantle, a leader's people need to believe that his support will always be there for them.

A Reciprocal Relationship

Why were Jesus' disciples loyal enough to Him to go victoriously into a den of lions, or to be burned alive, or to have their heads chopped off? How did it happen? Why do people continue to suffer persecution for their Christian faith rather than deny Christ and enjoy a season of relief?

What made the Apostle Paul, while he was facing death, write to his "beloved son" saying, *"God has not given us a spirit of fear, but of power and of love and of a sound mind. Therefore do not be ashamed of the testimony of our Lord, nor of me His prisoner, but share with me in the sufferings for the gospel according to the power of God"* (2 Timothy 1:2,7-8)?

Loyalty is not something you can receive without first giving of yourself. Jesus tells us why men and women are loyal to him: "I am the good shepherd. The good shepherd gives His life for the sheep" (John 10:11).

He is "good." This means He desires only good things for His sheep. He would and did give His very life for the good of His sheep. Nothing would stand in the way of a good outcome for them. He who owed no debt committed Himself, irrevocably, to pay the debt for those who couldn't pay it. He who was free allowed His heart to be chained to every other heart that would ever cry out in anguish for freedom from sin.

As managers, pastors, parents, spouses and teachers, we need to offer ourselves to our people. We need to give them our time, talents, energy, creativity, verbal and monetary praise, information and other life enriching resources. Because we want a heart commitment from them, we need to give them the same. Paul, writing to the Ephesians about the relationship between masters and servants, wrote, "Servants, be obedient to those who are your masters . . . with fear and trembling, in sincerity of heart, as to Christ; . . . doing the will of God from the heart, with good will doing service, as to the Lord, and not to men . . . *and you, masters, do the same things to them* . . . knowing that your own Master also is in heaven" (Ephesians 6:5-9). There must be a mutual expression of loyalty.

Turning The Pyramid Upside Down

MANTLE managers need to be an example, or a model, of the type of behavior we want to develop in our people. We need to be a showpiece to our employees, as Jesus was and is to His disciples. We must get them to listen by listening; to be loyal by being loyal; to respect by respecting. We need to display attributes such as admitting when we're wrong, being ready to change our minds, being teachable, showing mercy when mistakes are made, taking time to establish a caring relationship and keeping our word. These go a long way toward building loyalty within our workplaces, families, classrooms and churches. When discipline is required, those entrusted to us ought to know it will be administered. They should expect that good performers will be rewarded and others would not.

Have you ever worked for a manager who said, "Do it my way or hit the highway"? Have you ever heard a manager say, "You work for me," or "I'm the most important person in your life, and without me you're out of a job"?

Have you known a woman whose husband has wrongly used Bible verses to demand submission from her, rather than receiving it as a response to his love? If so, you'll be happy to know that this is wrong thinking and not biblical. Jesus' principle of servant-leadership is truth that improves the bottom line, because it makes workers, spouses, children, church members and students more loyal and committed to the organization than fear-leadership ever could.

"Turning the pyramid upside down" means that instead of fostering the belief that everyone works for the CEO and that management is most important, organizations are realizing that the front line is most important and everyone else works to make them the best they can be, because they touch the customer. A happy customer, research shows, will tell eight other potential customers. An unhappy customer will tell 16 others. The front line is now being empowered to do whatever it takes to delight the customer, and the entire management structure is geared to make that happen. This principle not only works for CEOs of companies, but also chief executives of churches, families, schools and other profit and non-profit organizations. Truly, the "greatest among you shall be your servant" (Matthew 23:11).

What are some practical ways that parents — especially fathers — can manifest servant-leadership and build loyalty in the home? Here's what Debra Fulghum Bruce identified in "The Worth of a Child" (*Pentecostal Evangel Magazine*, June 12, 1994):

Pray for children everywhere; Teach a personal faith in Jesus Christ; Consistently discipline the children as the Bible admonishes parents to do; Set high standards for the child, teaching him values and morals as he grows into adulthood; Talk with the child and really hear what he is saying; Budget the child's time so God and family are a priority over society's influence through television and video games.

Incidentally, wives and children can help build loyalty also. Wives can satisfy their husband's need for a companion and partner in what he enjoys doing; and children can respond to parents with appreciation.

In his book, *My Utmost for His Highest* (Oswald Chambers Publications Assn, Ltd., 1963), Chambers explains what it means to lose our lives for Christ, characterizing the MANTLE manager's commitment to those entrusted to him.

"I have been crucified with Christ; it is no longer I who live, but Christ lives in me" (Galatians 2:20). These words mean the breaking of my independence with my own hand and surrendering to the supremacy of the Lord Jesus. No one can do this for me; I must do it myself. God may bring me up to the point 365 times a year, but He cannot put me through it. It means breaking the husk of my individual independence of God, and emancipating my personality into oneness with Himself, not for my own ideas, but for absolute loyalty to Jesus. There's no possibility of dispute once I am there. The reality of the supernatural identification with Jesus Christ takes place at once, and the witness of the Spirit of God is unmistakable — "I have been crucified with Christ." The passion of Christianity is that I deliberately sign away my own rights and become a bond slave of Jesus Christ.

Fight An Unfair System

Another important attribute of the manager who builds loyalty with his people is that he fights an unfair system for them. He sometimes needs to "strike the Jordon river" as Elisha did with the mantle (2 Kings 2:14). Often there are unjust practices in companies that cause discouragement for our workers. These might be such things as how people are given promotions, practices of favoring one group over another for resource approvals, or granting overtime. Jesus fought against the system that the religious leaders imposed upon the people, that they themselves couldn't keep, and where the priests received a "kickback" from the sale of animals for the various sacrifices. He said, "It is written, 'My house is a house of prayer,' but you have made it a 'den of thieves'" (Luke 19:46).

On one Sabbath day, Jesus was walking with his disciples

through the corn. Because they were hungry, His disciples began to pluck the corn. When the Pharisees saw them, they told Jesus that they were breaking the Sabbath law. Jesus reminded them of how King David, when he was hungry, went right into the temple and ate the shewbread, which was not lawful, because it was reserved for the priests. Then He rebuked them for not understanding that God wanted mercy more than sacrifice; and, if they had understood this, they wouldn't be condemning the guiltless (Matthew 12: 1-8).

Managers, too, need to protect their people from abuse by business, school or church politics. We need to speak out against unjust systems of favoritism and "kickbacks" at the expense of worker morale and productivity.

THE MANTLE:
Challenges for the Church, the Home, and the School

BEING LOYAL & BUILDING LOYALTY

1. THE MANTLE CHURCH

a. Church leaders serve the members by lovingly coaching them through leadership, evangelism, teaching, counseling, parenting, worklife, etc. programs to make them better. Leaders put member interests and priorities before themselves.

b. Church policies are not made for the purpose of restricting the "abuser minority" but rather to benefit, enhance, and encourage the majority of the church members (e.g. a policy about using church resources).

c. There is an active leader visitation program to church member homes. They are visited at home or in the hospital when sick. Also, telephone contact, fellowship programs, and home Bible studies are used by church leaders to show their care for church members.

d. Church leaders are proactive and waste no time in correcting, disciplining or counseling those who

37

bring false teaching, immoral or abusive behavior into the church or into its families.

2. THE MANTLE HOME

a. Parents do not allow children to go undisciplined for improper behavior. They are careful not to favor one child over another in this area.
b. Parents are proactive in protecting their children against any corrupt, immoral or abusive behavior entering their lives from any source. Husbands and wives also protect and warn one another in each of these areas.
c. Parents recognize real accomplishments and reward their children equally.
d. Husbands and wives put each other's interests and priorities ahead of their own. They sacrifice for one another. Husbands provide financial security and affection to their wives. Wives provide admiration and good home-keeping for their husbands.

3. THE MANTLE SCHOOL

a. Teachers treat all students fairly in terms of discipline, grading, extra credit, privileges, homework and private tutoring.
b. Teachers and administrators are proactive in correcting, disciplining and counseling those who bring corrupt, immoral or abusive behavior into the school.
c. Administrators make teacher priorities come first.
d. Teachers sacrifice their own time to help students and work with parents.

Chapter Five
BUILDING UP OUR PEOPLE'S SELF-ESTEEM

When feeling ashamed or despondent, the mantle was a convenient thing to weep into or simply hide your face from the rest of the world. MANTLE managers offer a listening and learning opportunity for people to gain confidence and move ahead.

Fear And Micro-Management

Scripture tells us that "there is no fear in love; but perfect love casts out fear" (1 John 4:18).

A recent study of American business has shown that fear has a deep and negative effect on employee self-esteem. Workers lose trust and pride in their organization, dedication and commitment take a nose-dive; employees gravitate to destructive and defensive behavior in order to look out for "number one"; overly cautious people make more mistakes and want to hide them; and creativity bottoms out.

We need to treat people in a way that says, "You know your job, and you can be trusted to provide correct advice to me." We need to let workers — not managers — do their jobs. We must stop micro-managing people, making them afraid to do one creative thing on their own for fear of being "bloodied" — especially, if things go wrong. We must let people know we want more than their bodies. We want and need their intellect, their emotions, their heart and passion for excellence. Many people have "quit" inside. They don't believe in themselves anymore. We must convince them they still have the creative and productive juices to succeed.

Here's more from former foster child Christine Suguitan's story of how she came to value herself ("Healing for My Broken Heart," *Decision Magazine*, January 1994):

My new foster parents lavished me with compliments, acceptance — and time. I saw God more clearly than ever before. I sensed His love flowing from them to me. I felt wholly new. I was special. I had gifts and talents, and I mattered. The shell of worthlessness that I had worn all of my life began to dry like a husk and fall away. My healing wasn't swift. At times loneliness engulfed me. I would cry out to God in pain and wallow in the conviction that I was a nobody. Yet my foster parents continued with their encouragement, praise and love. I grew in courage and confidence. I was graduated from high school, excelled at an office job and was promoted to the position of secretary to the president of the company.

Jesus Builds Self-Esteem And Empowers His Disciples

In Luke 10, Jesus sends the 70 disciples out to various towns to witness. Verses 3 and 19 tell us that He trusted and had empowered them for the task. "Go your way; behold, I send you out as lambs among wolves." "Behold, I give you the authority to trample on serpents and scorpions, and over all the power of the enemy, and nothing shall by any means hurt you." Verse 17 tells us how they returned "with joy" and great self-esteem. In verse 18 Jesus immediately encourages them saying, "I saw Satan fall like lightning from heaven" — as if to say He saw Satan humbled by them.

This empowerment of Jesus' disciples didn't just happen. Jesus had to first tell them what He wanted them to do. He gave them directions. He then showed them how to do it — as a coach would. Jesus' disciples had observed Him as He cast out demons, healed the sick, and preached the good news to the poor. They were "coached" by the Master. Jesus had allowed them to practice what they learned and gave corrective guidance and encouragement. For example, when the disciples could not cast out a demon, He instructed them, "this kind does not go out except by prayer and fasting" (Matthew 17:21). When they were ready, He left them alone to "go forth." Here's His pattern:

Direct
Coach
Guide and encourage
Empower

Another example of Jesus' way to build self-esteem was shown after Peter denied Him three times before His crucifixion. After Jesus rose from the dead, the scripture says He told Mary, who saw Him first, to go tell His disciples and *Peter* (Mark 16:7) to meet Him in Galilee. Peter was ashamed and had wept bitterly over it. Jesus knew he felt bad enough but was concerned how the others felt about Peter. After all, Peter was the one who had stood up before them all and said he would never deny or desert the Lord. So Jesus confronted Peter, not alone, but in the presence of the others. He said, "Do you love Me more than these?" (John 21:15). The word Jesus used for "love" was *agape* —an unselfish love that asks for no love in return. Peter's answer was that he did love the Lord, but his word for "love" was *phileo* — a brother to brother love; not an unselfish love at all. Peter was admitting that his love fell short of what it should be. That showed the others that Peter was no longer the cocky, prideful, "better than everyone else" person he used to be. Then Jesus, with everyone hearing, still told Peter to "feed my lambs" (John 21:15). That went on three times. Jesus made it clear to Peter and the others that Peter was still a very useful and important part of the ministry.

Most people who have made a mistake or acted inappropriately already know it. It doesn't have to be crammed down their throats again. We need to learn as MANTLE managers to use the appropriate firmness and tact to offer constructive criticism and correction. Its aim should be to maintain or build up our people's self-esteem. Remember when Jesus told us to "visit those in prison" (Matthew 25)? I believe there are many in prisons without bars — prisons of the "uninspired," the "unmotivated," and "low self-esteem." We need, indeed, to visit them with support and encouragement.

Jezebel wanted to even the score with Elijah, who'd just slain 450 of her prophets after a mighty test of whether the Lord was God or if Baal was God (1 Kings 18:21-40). She ordered Elijah to be killed, and Elijah ran from her. He was afraid and didn't display that faith with which he honored God on Mount Carmel against the prophets of Baal. He even requested the Lord to take his life, but God still provided food and shelter for him as he ran. Finally, after forty days and nights, Elijah found himself in a cave at Mount Horeb, where the Lord asked, "What are you doing here, Elijah?" (1 Kings 19:9).

God patiently heard Elijah's complaints. Then God said, "Go out, and stand on the mountain before the Lord" (1Kings 19:11). God then demonstrated His mighty power by sending a great wind, then an earthquake, and then a fire; but Elijah didn't find God in those demonstrations of power. After the fire, God sent a "still small voice." Elijah found God in the still small voice, and he hid his face (I believe because he was ashamed of himself) in his mantle. After listening to Elijah again, God told him to "return on your way" (1 Kings 19:15), and Elijah was restored and prepared to do his Master's work again.

MANTLE management doesn't overpower people into admitting their mistakes, but offers a listening and learning opportunity for people to gain confidence and press on. Among other things, it's important that we offer a great deal of education and training to those entrusted to us. Often, we supply technology to people without adequate training, and instead of building them up, we succeed in making them feel ignorant because they can't adequately use the new technology. I also believe that we should let people learn whatever they want. Most often in the business world, it will be something related to the job for advancement; but if it isn't directly job related, it will still benefit the company. Many are in a rut because of the day-to-day routine — and training will get their brains out of the rut and energized again. When they return to work, the cost of training is compensated by happier and more productive workers.

Building Self-Esteem In Your Spouse

MANTLE manager husbands can build up self-esteem in their wives by taking time to talk with them. As Willard F. Harley Jr., Ph.D., licensed clinical psychologist, said in his book, *His Needs Her Needs* (Revell, 1986):

I rarely have a man ask me, "Why isn't my wife talking to me?" but I often hear from women, "Why isn't my husband talking to me?" Women seem to enjoy conversation for its own sake. Many women will spend hours with each other on the telephone, while men rarely call each other just to chat and be brought up-to-date. Meetings and luncheons and other gatherings where the entire purpose seems to be talking about their personal concerns bring women much pleasure. When men gather in conclaves, they tend to talk about practical matters, like fixing cars, the best place to fish, or who holds first place on the sport of that season. They also like to exchange jokes and anecdotes, but they tend not to talk about themselves or their feelings.

If a husband seriously wants to meet his wife's need to feel close to him, he will give the task sufficient time and attention. I tell male clients they should learn to set aside as much as 15 hours a week to give their wives undivided attention. Many men look at me as if they think I'm losing my mind, or they just laugh and say, "In other words, I need a 36-hour day." I don't bat an eye, but simply ask them how much time they spent giving their wives undivided attention during their courting days. Any bachelor who fails to devote something close to 15 hours a week to his girlfriend faces a strong likelihood of losing her. When a courting couple shares their time, they usually have some basic, although possibly unconscious goals. They try to get to know each other more thoroughly and let each other know how much they care. Why should these goals be dropped after the wedding? The couple desiring a happy marriage carries on with these functions and goals after the wedding. Primarily for the sake of the woman, they must set aside time to have dates with each other. . . . Caring partners communicate in a caring way.

In the same book, Harley gives guidelines for wives to meet the needs of their husbands by remaining attractive — to be the wives they originally married — and for fulfilling them sexually. These are also needed to build the husband's self-esteem.

Another important behavior for wives who reverence their husbands, and for all MANTLE managers, is to demonstrate "belief in" our people. We need to get this right. The best way to explain it is by using a song sung by Kenny Rogers, "She Believes in Me." It's about a nightclub singer who has just sung his heart out and returns from the club in the wee hours of the morning very tired and hungry. His wife is in bed, and he tries not to wake her. He confesses that he told her that if she'd be his girl, he'd change the world for them with his little songs, but it didn't happen. He failed to create the tune that would go to the top of the charts! As he enters the kitchen for a bite to eat, he spots his guitar standing there like a "secret friend." And though worn out from the very ordinary, expected and unexciting night at the club, he picks up that guitar, attempting to create another melody that might still "change the world." He does this, he says, because "she believes in me."

Wives — and all MANTLE managers — need to be

especially "tuned in" to opportunities to show how they really "believe in" those entrusted to them. Not only will this help build self-esteem, but it will make those entrusted kick even harder to reach "finish lines" that they would normally have felt were just out of reach for them.

THE MANTLE:
Challenges for the Church, the Home, and the School

BUILDING UP OUR PEOPLE'S SELF-ESTEEM

1. THE MANTLE CHURCH

   a. The overall church leadership model is one of servant-leader not micro manager or fear manager. Trust between leaders and church members inspires active participation by the majority. Manipulation techniques are not needed.

   b. Leaders lovingly take members through the stages (direction, coaching, encouragement) leading to empowerment for active decision-making, participation in church activities, and for representing the church.

   c. Deacons (or other "officials") are truly elected from among the current church members by other members with little or no "filtering out" by the current Board or the Pastor.

2. THE MANTLE HOME

   a. Parents correct their children in a way that says "I love you and want you to know right from wrong." Parents are under control when discipline is given so that children do not fear their parents, even though they know they will be punished for improper behavior.

   b. Parents don't jump to conclusions about their children's behavior but listen to them and use every opportunity to teach them. Husbands and wives trust one another, and always presume the best about each other.

c. After taking children through "direction," "coaching" and "encouraging" in a particular area, parents trust their children and give them independence in that area.

d. Husbands and wives encourage one another to pursue their "dreams" for improving themselves (e.g. education, job, write a book, etc.). They sacrifice themselves to let this happen.

3. THE MANTLE SCHOOL

a. Teachers find opportunities to give students independent study assignments. Prior to this, they (1) give them directions, (2) assign preliminary work, and (3) provide feedback on the results, which includes encouragement and compliments when earned.

b. Administrators let the teachers teach and avoid micromanaging their classrooms. Teachers are empowered with special assignments in their fields or in growth areas (e.g. counseling) which give them special recognition with students, faculty and parents.

c. Teachers don't presume bad behavior on the part of students but lend a listening ear. They use every opportunity to teach students about themselves and how to be successful in life.

Chapter Six
BUILDING UNITY AND FAMILY

*The **mantle** was the symbol of the office of a prophet. That symbol was often used to perform a wonderworking act to demonstrate that the power was in the office, not the individual.*

Creating Teams That Care Like Families
With the downsizing of many organizations today and the flattening of hierarchies by eliminating middle management, there's a lot of emphasis on teamwork. Employees need to learn, not only to be individually productive, but to foster productivity in teammates who are partners with them in the enterprise. They need to begin evaluating their own success by the success of the team.

A MANTLE manager needs to build a unity of purpose into many diverse (and usually self-reliant) individuals and empower them to act decisively in his behalf as a team. In the following description of 2 Kings 2:8, we see the mantle analogy to this empowerment:

> And now the two (Elijah and Elisha) had gone down to the bank of the Jordan, and stood by the edge of its waters. Elijah took off his loose upper garment (e.g. the mantle), the symbol of his office, and wrapping it together as if to make it a staff (compare Exodus 14:16) smote the waters with it. And lo, as when the Ark of God had preceded Israel (Joshua 4:23), the waters divided and they passed over dry-shod. Surely there could not

have been a more apt teaching for Elisha for all future times, that the power of wonderworking rested not with the prophet individually, but was attached to his office(e.g. the prophetic team) of which this rough raiment was the badge (Alfred Edersheim, M.A. (OXON), D.D., Ph.D., Fleming Revell Co. New York, 1985).

When Elisha then took up the mantle of Elijah (2 Kings 2:13), his having the mantle was proof that he was vested with the authority and influence of his master.

There are various team approaches employed in the workplace to improve productivity today. One team is called the "natural work team," consisting of people who normally work together. Another is called the "cross-functional team," consisting of people who might not directly work together every day, but the work of one member eventually affects the other. The benefit of teaming these people is to improve the overall process by broadening their knowledge base.

A variation of both of these is to take a natural work group or a cross-functional team and make it "self-directed." This team has no permanent leader, but instead allows the team to bestow authority on various members to accomplish functions that were previously done by a supervisor, such as assigning work to other members, developing the budget, or prioritizing work. Another team, which is often used to improve processes and maximize the work of a smaller work force, is the "process action team." This team generally meets weekly for an hour or two and could be cross-functional or work together everyday.

In each case, teams are generally given a set of tools and techniques to use — normally with the help of a trained facilitator — to help them make accurate decisions. These include: Statistical Process Control, Fishbone Diagrams, Paredo Charts, Brainstorming, and Plus, Minus, Interesting, to mention just a few. A lot of effort and money goes into training team members to function well as a team, especially how to deal with differences of opinions and interaction between members whose personalities differ. When a team has completed its deliberations on a problem, it generally presents its results to management for approval. Then it proceeds with implementation. As important as teaming is for maximizing productivity, we still fall far short of what could be realized if management doesn't create a climate of "family" and supplement the colder, mechanical business processes with an attitude of mutual care that permeates the organization.

"Then Elijah passed by him (Elisha) and threw his mantle on him" (1 Kings 19:19). Besides calling him to the prophetic office, the mantle provided a sense of warmth and a sense of belonging to the "family" of prophets (since he was wearing the "badge" of the prophet).

The teaming, especially cross-functional teaming, sends a good message to everyone — that others need me to do my job properly, and that I am an important part of the whole. This concept can be illustrated, as the Apostle Paul does in 1 Corinthians 12:14-20, as the parts of a human body that depend upon each other. "For in fact the body is not one member but many. If the foot should say, 'Because I am not a hand, I am not of the body,' is it therefore not of the body? . . . But now God has set the members, each one of them, in the body just as He pleased... But now indeed there are many members, yet one body."

The concept of interdependence, however, is not enough. We need to develop the idea of *family*, including a sense of identification with others, where members care about one another. The scripture is replete with references to members of Christ's Body, the Church, being "brothers and sisters." It also speaks often of our responsibilities to care for one another in various ways. "Be kindly affectionate to one another with brotherly love, in honor giving preference to one another" (Romans 12:10). In other places we are told to pray, warn, greet, care for, be hospitable, bear with one another and to bear one another's burdens. A very affectionate reference to family caring is made by the Apostle Paul to the church members at Thessalonica when he said, "But we were gentle among you, just as a nursing mother cherishes her own children" (1 Thessalonians 2:7). Paul, their true spiritual servant-leader head of family, cared for them like a mother who nurses her child at her breast.

This feeling of family caring can be fostered by a MANTLE manager remembering employee birthdays with cards or remembering someone who's sick with a get well card or telephone call to encourage them. For employees who are hospitalized, a visit by the supervisor (who brings along fellow workers) can sometimes do more for recovery than the doctor. This family feeling is also fostered when a manager promotes the idea of one part of the organization helping other parts — making it a priority of management for resources (money and people) from one organizational element to be supplied to another in time of real need. Upper management must foster a cross-organization view that says to everyone, "When one part of the organization hurts, we all hurt and will help." In many organizations, managers feel threatened about volunteering their people to help, fearing their people will be taken away from them. In these organizations, they better show they have more than enough work for their own groups. It's unthinkable to assist another group. Hence the attitude of "My four and no more" is fostered. Instead, we should cross-train our people so they can do at least one other employee's job and consider the manager who "gives up his people" as a good manager of his resources instead of "not having enough work to do."

Upper management's attitude needs to change to "If you help, I won't consider you 'fat' just 'helpful,' and I'll take the temporary 'heat' if you miss a service or product delivery date." In the long haul, managers win by creating feelings of unity and camaraderie, even if in the short term a customer must be "delayed" or "put off" temporarily in order to serve our own people. Over time, customer service will improve with this approach because of the synergism caused by creating unity and real teamwork as well as building loyalty with your people.

Jesus knew the importance and powerful effect of the unity of believers. In His prayer to the Father before the crucifixion He said, "Now I am no longer in the world, but these (His disciples) are in the world, and I come to You. Holy Father, keep through Your name those whom You have given Me, that they may be one as We are . . . . that they all may be one, as You, Father, are in Me, and I in You; that they also may be one in Us; that the world may believe that You sent Me" (John 17:11,21).

He went on to say that He had given them the ability to be one. He had empowered them to become perfect in their unity. This was done so that the rest of the onlooking world would realize that Jesus was sent from the Father (John 17:22,23). MANTLE managers need to provide the policies, attitudes, training and overall work environment that will empower our people to work as one.

The Family Unit

What about families that aren't functioning as families? What must be done to build unity there? How can we begin to empower families to work as teams? MANTLE fathers must exercise the servant-leader role with their children.

We need to pray for our children and teach a personal faith in Jesus. We need to be consistent in discipline and set high moral values. We need to take time to hear what they have to say and budget their time properly. We also need to stick with the empowerment pattern given in Chapter Five: *Give Direction, Coach, Guide and Encourage, and Empower.* We can't go from *direction to empowerment,* skipping *coaching and encouraging.* We need to take our children through each step. Wives have their part to do also. They need to satisfy their husbands' need for domestic support by cooking, washing, ironing, cleaning, calling repair people, and attending to the basic needs of the children.

Unity In The Church

What's the unity that our churches should be demonstrating to the world? How can MANTLE pastors and other church leaders develop that unity in church members? There are actually four aspects to the unity of churches: unity with God, unity among church members, unity with other churches, and unity with non-Christians (e.g. those potential future members of the Christian community).

Unity with God comes when we accept Jesus as our Savior — as the sacrifice for our sin. "Therefore, if anyone is in Christ, he is a new creation; old things have passed away; behold, all things have become new" (2 Corinthians 5:17). "He (Jesus) came to His own, and His own did not receive Him. But as many as received Him, to them He gave the right to become children of God, even to those who believe in His name: who were born, not of blood, nor of the will of the flesh, nor of the will of man, but of God" (John 1:11-13). We become members of God's family. This unity is the beginning, initiated by God Himself, not only for us, individually, but also to reach out and build unity with others.

Crucial is our developing a oneness with our fellow local church members. If we don't have unity with our own church members, how can we hope to have unity with other churches or with those unchurched? As briefly mentioned earlier in this chapter, the scriptures speak of brothers and sisters in Christ loving one another (Romans 13:8), accepting one another (Romans 15:7), preferring one another (Romans 12:10), bearing one another's burdens (Galatians 6:2,5), bearing with one another (Ephesians 4:2), being members one of another (Ephesians 4:25), building up and encouraging one another (Romans 14:19).

MANTLE pastors need to provide opportunities for church members to meet in small groups after teaching their congregations about real fellowship — what it really means to share Christ and to have a mutual care for one another. Pastors and other church leaders must emphasize that church members should *not* look first at the differences in others — that's what the world does — but should *first* recognize their commonality of purpose. He can do this by teaching about interdependence and the need we each have for the gifts and abilities that God has given to each church member. Without every member using the gift he received from the Lord to benefit others, the church can't hope to develop "to a perfect man, to the measure of the stature of the fullness of Christ" (Ephesians 4:13).

On one occasion while Jesus was preaching in a house, four men broke through the rooftop to lower before Him a sick man on a stretcher (Luke 5:17-26). Sometimes members of the church are in need — sort of "on the stretcher." Just like the sick man, these church members don't care who's holding the left, right, top or bottom of the stretcher. They only care about getting their need to Jesus! All of us need to be "stretcher bearers" for one another by using our God-given abilities.

Besides preaching and teaching, by his own example, a pastor can recognize everybody's birthday or wedding anniversary — perhaps singing "Happy Birthday" or "Happy Anniversary" to them in the congregation if it falls on a church meeting day. Everybody deserves a visit from him in their home or at the hospital. Everybody can be given opportunities for growth and ministry. The pastor should demonstrate that "Everybody is somebody!"

Jesus empowered believers with the Holy Spirit and gave us the power to become *one* (John 17:23). He did this so that the *world* would know that His heavenly Father sent Him and loves them as He loves Jesus. Jesus meant that as *all* believers demonstrated oneness to the world, it would convince unbelievers that Jesus was indeed sent to save them. For this to happen today, Christians of different denominations need to develop and demonstrate this *visible* unity. MANTLE pastors and church leaders, without compromising their own beliefs, need to stop emphasizing denominational differences and encourage participation in cross-denominational activities. They can encourage people from their respective churches to get together with other churches to feed the poor, clothe the naked, visit the sick, and evangelize. The Billy Graham Crusades are excellent examples of how cross-denominational church members team up to pray *together*, take evangelism classes *together*, and work *together* to mobilize their church resources for reaching their greater metropolitan area with the Gospel of the Lord Jesus Christ.

That spirit of cooperation needs to become a normal, expected, regular practice of individual believers and churches. We are co-laborers with each other and Christ in the work of evangelizing. Perhaps we need to "co-picnic," "co-softball," or "co-breakfast" locally with other churches, so together we can "co-operate" and "co-labor."

Believers must understand that they need their brothers and sisters of other denominations to become mature in Christ. Believers need to see that God has set in each local church those He wants there to accomplish His purposes. However, we also must unite ourselves to the Church that's bigger than the walls of our own buildings. We need to say, "Though I am a Baptist, I am *first* a Christian," "Though I am a Methodist, I am *first* a Christian," or "Though I am a Pentecostal, I am *first* a Christian." A major element of evangelizing the world is that the *whole* Church be one — one in the purpose of reaching the lost, in caring for one another and satisfying all the "one another" scriptures cited above — to love, accept, prefer, bear burdens, bear with, be members of, build up, and encourage one another. When believers understand and practice this oneness of purpose with believers of other denominations, then identification with the yet unbelieving world (the fourth unity) will become more of a priority and reality for believers. The real *agape* love developed by caring for those who may be a different denomination will overflow to those like we were before we accepted Christ as Savior. "God demonstrates His own love toward us, in that, while we were still sinners, Christ died for us" (Romans 5:8).

BUILDING UNITY AND FAMILY

1. THE MANTLE CHURCH

    a. Church leaders teach from the Word about unity in its four dimensions: within your church; across other local churches; upward as fellow workers and family of the Lord; and outward to the unsaved.

    b. Church leaders bring church members with them to visit other sick church members.

    c. Church members and leaders are cross-trained to fill in for others when needed (e.g. Sunday school teachers, ushers, leaders of music, prayer, worship, etc.)

    d. Many informal church gatherings provide fellowship and sharing time.

2. THE MANTLE HOME

    a. Parents show their children how much they need each other as a family. Parents help children with homework. Big brother or sister helps little brother or sister with homework. Children are given specific tasks to do in the home and all family members benefit. Children are instructed to help their brother or sister with a task, when the other is sick.

    b. Husbands and wives back each other up. Dad learns how to do the cooking when Mom is not available. Mom learns how to mow the lawn. Everybody learns how to use the computer to help one another.

    c. Parents, husbands and wives make birthdays, anniversaries and holidays become special family traditions.

    d. Parents develop a calendar for the family that shows the activities of each family member. Everyone tries to attend these events. When children mature and are geographically separated, parents continue to produce and distribute the calendar to maintain family unity.

e. Parents and children support one another during hard times (e.g. suffering or mourning). Parents take time to explain the circumstances to children and comfort them with hugs and kisses. Parents give priority time and energy to their children.

f. Parents, husbands and wives sacrifice for one another and the children.

3. THE MANTLE SCHOOL

a. Teachers use the calendar to celebrate special days as a class. Everyone gets a task to do for the day that will contribute to the celebration. If appropriate, teachers invite the class to their home for a particular event (e.g. a special English class can celebrate Robert Burns' birthday with a Scottish "haggis").

b. Teachers and administrators look for opportunities to create teams for special projects, especially teacher-student teams (e.g. the Yearbook Team, the Graduation Ceremony Team, the Parent-Teacher Visitation Team, the Student Council Team, etc.).

c. Give the responsibility for a field trip to the class. Allow them to decide what jobs need to be done and to vote for the students to accomplish those jobs.

d. Teachers bring students with them to visit a student who is sick or hospitalized. Administrators bring fellow teachers to visit sick or hospitalized faculty.

Chapter Seven
GOOD COMMUNICATIONS AND PLANNING

The prophets, who were identified by that peculiar garb called a mantle, made of skins dressed with the hair on them, were God's vessels to communicate His messages and plans.

Communications

After 30 years of government service, I've concluded that the complaint most often heard from employees is that management doesn't tell them what's happening. There's always a feeling that the supervisor knows things that he isn't sharing with his people to maintain some control or power over them. Whether true or not, it is the perception of the people that really matters.

As a MANTLE manager servant-leader, we want to be "peculiar" in keeping our people informed about every aspect of work life, home life, and church life. These people are the stockholders of our businesses and the stakeholders of our non-profit enterprises.

Because we're encouraging their ideas and looking for continuous improvement through teaming, it's essential that those entrusted to us be well informed to make knowledgeable recommendations and decisions. Open and honest communications should be our way of life. Employees should be told about everything that could concern them:

- How's the company doing financially?
- What's the quality and timeliness of our product and service like from the customers' point of view?
- How's their individual performance contributing to the bottom line?
- Who's our competition and how are they doing?
- Who's being rewarded and for what reasons?
- Is anything happening to cause downsizing?

Some managers criticize this openness, worrying that people will become nervous, which will reduce their effectiveness. The reality is that, if employees don't hear what's happening from their own supervisor, they'll hear something — perhaps true or perhaps false — from the company rumor mill, which is worse than just hearing the truth. We need to respect our people by giving them information that impacts their lives. If there are some who will freeze up rather than be set free by hearing the truth, then we need to know who these people are and work with them one-on-one.

The Apostle Paul's communication to the churches was so important. In some cases, the churches were being misinformed by false teachers, and the people needed to be reminded of the truth. "O foolish Galatians! Who has bewitched you that you should not obey the truth" (Galatians 3:1). At other times, he needed to give them knowledge they didn't have. "Now concerning spiritual gifts, brethren, I do not want you to be ignorant" (1 Corinthians 12:1). "Brethren, do not be children in understanding; however in malice be babes, but in understanding be mature" (1 Corinthians 14:20). At other times, he needed to correct or warn against certain behavior. For example, when the Corinthians were arguing about the propriety of eating meat offered to idols, Paul instructed, "But food does not commend us to God; for neither if we eat are we the better, nor if we do not eat are we the worse. But beware lest somehow this liberty of yours become a stumbling block to those who are weak . . . And because of your knowledge shall the weak brother perish, for whom Christ died?" (1 Corinthians 8: 8-11).

Consider some examples of how Jesus communicated. His Sermon on the Mount (Matthew 5, 6, 7) is considered by psychologists to be the most concise statement of the most important truths for practical living and a sound mind ever given — although some of it may not be easy to swallow. In three chapters, He advised about:

- How to be happy and make a difference
- How to have an influence on others
- The importance of God's Word
- What our spiritual standards should be
- The importance of inward purity
- The sacredness of marriage
- The importance of keeping our word
- The ignorance of profanity
- The need for forbearance with those who hurt or insult us
- The need for unselfish love and unlimited service
- Benevolence
- How to pray and fast
- Divine providence and what to do about worry
- Judging others
- The two ways to live — one leading to heaven and the other to death
- How to know what's good from what's evil
- How to build a solid foundation for living

The importance of communicating truth to people can be seen in another example of Jesus speaking to two disciples on the road to Emmaus (Luke 24:13-33). Jesus died and rose and now approached the disciples as they were discussing the troubling events of His death. They were dejected because they had hoped that it was He (referring to Jesus) who was going to redeem Israel. They did not know that Jesus had been resurrected and with their faith so low did not even recognize Him in His resurrected body. So, He expounded to them, from all the scriptures beginning at Moses and all the Prophets, the things concerning Himself, showing them how Christ had to suffer these things. As He spoke to them, their faith grew; and after He sat eating with them, as He took bread, blessed it, broke it, and gave it to them, their eyes were opened; and they recognized Him. They went from dejected to happy and useful disciples because Jesus opened their eyes with the truth. Similarly, our employees, family members, and church members will become more useful and productive when the truth is presented in an understandable way. Paul cautions in Ephesians 4:15 that we must speak the truth in love. This is how Jesus ministered the truth to these disciples — in the way that they could receive it and appreciate it.

We're especially concerned today with family break-ups. In her article, "How to Adultery Proof Your Marriage" (*Woman's Touch Magazine*, July/August 1994), Lonnie Collins Pratt explains the necessity of good communication:

Begin by talking to your spouse. Ask how he feels about your spending time with male co-workers and friends. If your work involves business trips, ask if he is concerned about it. Invite his opinion of your friends and welcome his input. Talk about how much intimacy is too much. Are there certain things neither of you should discuss with friends of the opposite sex? How will you know when intimacy has reached a danger point in friendship? For example, in an intimate relationship, you would know someone's daily schedule, their dreams, and their fears. You would be able to answer questions from others such as: "Where is Jon?", "What was Jon thinking when he did that?" or "What will Jon be doing tomorrow?" Though it's possible you could generally know this information in a good friendship, the more details a person exposes about his life, the more intimate the relationship grows.

Throughout the history of Israel, we find that God often communicated His guidance, direction, and correction through a prophet — except for the period between Malachi and Matthew, when God was silent. He was faithful to them even when they didn't follow His words.

Jesus said, before His crucifixion, that He wouldn't leave us comfortless but would send His Spirit to be in us, and He (the Holy Spirit) would lead us into all truth (John 14:18,26; 16:13). He is faithful today to speak to us through His Spirit and His Word. He does not leave us comfortless. Likewise, we must faithfully communicate openly to our people, to give them security and comfort in the belief that we can be trusted to let them know what's happening.

Planning

Often, management is guilty of having no goals and objectives; so an employee is left with a feeling of aimlessness. He keeps trying to contribute objectives to management to satisfy his natural need for security. Management needs an action plan to keep in the forefront of people's minds. The scripture warns, "Where there is no vision, the people perish" (Proverbs 29:18 KJV).

Employees need to know where they're going and what their contribution will be. Church members need to know what the church's emphasis will be over the coming year. Husbands and wives, parents and children need to know what major directions, changes and goals will affect them. What will they learn or develop into over time? We're each developing into someone as time passes, and we should each have an opportunity to know what that person might be like and make career choices accordingly. Our people need to feel that they've contributed to the goals of their organization. The process of goal-setting needs to be highly participative to (1) make people feel they are valued members and (2) motivate them to support achieving the goal.

One of those mantle-wearing prophets, Jeremiah, assured the people of God's vision for them and His openness to their input: "For I know the thoughts that I think toward you (some translations say "plans I have for you"), says the Lord, thoughts of peace and not of evil, to give you a future and a hope. Then you will call upon Me and go and pray to Me, and I will listen to you. And you will seek Me and find Me, when you search for Me with all your heart" (Jeremiah 29:11-13).

The entire Bible, God's Word, is His revealed plan for salvation for all — not Jews or Gentiles alone. It's God's plan, His guidebook, for saving all souls from eternal death and giving them eternal life through Christ. Though we didn't know it, we most definitely contributed to this plan because we "all have sinned and fall short of the glory of God" (Romans 3:23), so "death spread to all men" (Romans 5:12). "But God demonstrates His own love toward us, in that while we were still sinners, Christ died for us" (Romans 5:8). "For the wages of sin is death, but the gift of God is eternal life in Christ Jesus our Lord" (Romans 6:23). So our sin brings us to the plan God ordained for our salvation.

Disciples of Jesus choose to be His disciples. They understand what is required of them (see Matthew 28:18-20, Acts 1:4-8) and what they are promised to become (see Ephesians 4:13-16). He involves them in goal-setting. "Ask, and it will be given to you; seek, and you will find; knock, and it will be opened to you" (Matthew 7:7).

"Then He said to His disciples, 'The harvest truly is plentiful, but the laborers are few. Therefore pray the Lord of the harvest to send out laborers into His harvest'" (Matthew 9:37,38). Their prayer becomes input to the goal of reaching the lost and also moves them to become involved in that process themselves.

These are examples of general plans; but we also find Jesus giving specific plans for His apostles' lives. Paul is told of God's plan for him as he traveled on the road to Damascus (Acts 26:12-18); and Peter is told of God's plan for his life (John 21:18). Likewise, we managers should have general plans and a vision for our entire organization, as well as specific plans for individuals (e.g. individual development plans).

The plans we have should not be so far into the future that our people have trouble visualizing them happening. The Apostle Paul used an example of running a race when he said, "forgetting those things which are behind and reaching forward to those things which are ahead, I press toward the goal for the prize of the upward call of God in Christ Jesus" (Philippians 3:13,14). The race was laid out. He could see his way clearly. The prize was "that I may know Him" (Philippians 3:10). He could visualize being like Christ someday; and just like a miler who "kicks" hardest when the finish line is in sight, Paul pressed toward the goal. Our people ought to be "runners" who can see the finish line and are kicking to reach it. That's when their hearts are really into the race and their productivity is the greatest.

THE MANTLE:
Challenges for the Church, the Home, and the School

GOOD COMMUNICATIONS AND PLANNING

1. THE MANTLE CHURCH

   a. Every aspect of church life affecting the members is communicated to them when it happens and regularly throughout the year — not just at annual Board meetings. Communications can take place in various ways: fellowship meetings, Sunday morning bulletins, church letters, telephone chains, etc. Some questions to answer for church members are: How does the church stand financially in the various categories? How are the outreach ministries doing? How are church activities doing (Sunday school, children's church, the Christian school ministry, the benevolence ministry, prayer requests and answers to prayer)? Where is help needed? How do we serve the surrounding communities?

b. Members are surveyed about their thoughts on goals for the local church. Church leaders try to incorporate these into next year's planning.

2. THE MANTLE HOME

a. Everything affecting the home is communicated to and by its members regularly. Dinner time, or whenever the whole family gathers, is the best time. Some discussion ideas follow: What upcoming events will family be involved with? What community and world events are affecting our lives? How're family finances? Any changes? Have any family members been recognized, praised or criticized? Anything happening with our friends or community that we can help with? Any difficulty in school, church, the workplace or at home?
b. Husbands and wives share intimately about their lives at home, work and church, as well as children, money and sex. If disagreements cannot be resolved, they agree to make it a matter of personal and joint prayer.
c. Husbands and wives both contribute to the family goals and activities for the upcoming year. Parents encourage contributions from children on their expectations and try to incorporate these into family plans.

3. THE MANTLE SCHOOL

a. Teachers communicate to students what will help them grow academically or as a better teammate. (e.g. study books or after-hours tutoring available, classes being started, clubs/teams and students recognized lately, financial aid tips).
b. Administrators inform teachers how they can advance and can be recognized as outstanding achievers.
c. Teachers listen (formally and informally) to students' expectations and try to incorporate their goals into class plans. Administrators do the same for their teachers.

Chapter Eight
RECOGNIZING AND REWARDING GOOD PERFORMANCE

When employees or teams have "taken up the mantle" of their managers and have performed in a manner that demonstrates they have taken special "ownership" or responsibility for their work, then a reward should be given. Matthew 10:41 says, "He who receives a prophet in the name of a prophet shall receive a prophet's reward."

People Behind The Scenes

I recently read an item in *Our Daily Bread* (October 1993), titled "The Cost of Giving Support," which described how in 1989, paraplegic Mark Wellman climbed the sheer granite face of Yosemite's El Capitan. On the last day of his climb, *The Fresno Bee* ran a picture of Wellman being carried triumphantly on the shoulders of climbing companion Mike Corbett. The caption read, "Paraplegic and partner prove no wall is too high to climb."

What the story did not say was that in helping Wellman scale El Capitan once, Corbett had to make that difficult, demanding ascent three times! The *Our Daily Bread* item also pointed out that there was a lot more to the story of Moses having his hands upheld to bring victory by God's help in a crucial battle (Exodus 17:8-16). It was the two, Aaron and Hur, who had to climb a mountain, use their strength, and make the commitment to support Moses' arms. The message is that people who serve behind the scenes often pay a higher price than those who are in the center of public attention. Many managers look good because their people behind the scenes have done a great job. They should be recognized and rewarded. The Apostle Paul realized that supporting him, while he was a prisoner, took sacrifice on the part of certain people; and he recognized their contributions and rewarded them by "publicly" mentioning their support of him in writing to the Colossian church (Colossians 4:7-11).

Rewarding People Properly

Incentives for good performance can take many forms. It's important for the MANTLE manager to know his people well enough to "fit" the reward to the person. Jesus said, "I am the good shepherd; and I know My sheep, and am known by My own" (John 10:14). After all, Jesus didn't heal the blind man's legs!

As managers, we need to use instruments like Myers-Briggs tests not only to know how to communicate with people better but also to reward them better. For example, if you wanted to give an employee a choice assignment as a reward, you wouldn't give an "introvert" an assignment that requires interaction with a lot of people. You also wouldn't give an "extrovert" an assignment that has no interaction, or a "thinker" assignment to a "feeler."

Many managers wait until the end of a performance period to give rewards. That's not all bad, but it certainly doesn't go far enough. We also need to reward people as soon after the actual accomplishment as possible.

Jesus has rewards awaiting us in heaven. He also rewards us in the short term. The "heavenly" rewards are mentioned in scripture as "crowns" and will be given at a huge award ceremony called the "bema judgment"or "the judgment seat of Christ" (2 Corinthians 5:10). These awards are mentioned in scripture:

- "Crown of life" for those withstanding tribulation(Revelation 2:10)
- "Crown of glory" for elders and pastors (1 Peter 5:1-4)
- "Crown of rejoicing" for faithfully witnessing(1 Thessalonians 2:19)
- "Crown of righteousness" for those who long for Christ's return (2 Timothy 4:8)
- "Incorruptible crown" for victors of the daily spiritual struggle (1 Corinthians 9:25)

We too should have award ceremonies that bring all our people together and distribute the various awards. We've found that a quarterly award ceremony helps promote both unity and motivation. Besides the "end-of-performance" awards, however, we've recognized our people as quickly after the actual accomplishment as we could. Whenever the check for a monetary award arrives, we give it to them privately and then present the certificate at the quarterly ceremony. We've found that creating a balance between humorous and serious awards is important to achieve the results of creating a family atmosphere while acknowledging individual contributions.

I asked 30 Christians to tell me how Jesus rewards them as they live their lives day-to-day. Everyone agreed that His presence was reward enough, but here are some other responses regarding what Jesus gives as rewards:

- Responsibility (Matthew 25:29)
- The desire of our hearts (Psalm 37:4; 107:9)
- All our needs (Philippians 4:6,19)
- His approval by the anointing (Psalm 23:5)
- The benefit of being part of His family (Romans 12:10,13,16; Ephesians 4:32)
- Material blessings (Matthew 6:33; 19:29)
- Answers to our requests (Matthew 7:7)
- Encouragement (Luke 10:17-20)
- Forgiveness (John 21:15-17)

- The Holy Spirit and empowerment for service (John 16:13)
- He loves us as we are, while He shapes us into what He wants us to be (John 15:13)

MANTLE managers of people — whether managers of businesses, churches, schools or families — need to recognize and reward people for their accomplishments. This might be as simple as saying, "Thanks for doing a good job"; or it may be a special assignment, training, a monetary award, or certificate.

In our homes, husbands can recognize their wives in as many ways as their creativity and budget will allow. Giving sincere compliments and telling her "I love you" at least once a day are good starting points. Wives also need to honestly admire their husbands. They must appreciate them for what they are already — not for what they expect them to become someday. Parents need to do the same for their children.

Everyone needs to feel appreciated — to get a "gold star" or win the game ball — as they pursue excellence in their lives. The rewards shouldn't become expected for ordinary performance but should motivate people to extraordinary support. We need to send a message to people that when they "stretch themselves" for us, we take notice. We will recognize it — not just at the end of the performance period but whenever the deed is done. We need to catch people doing something right and praise them for it because that's the performance that they will then repeat. With downsizing in business upon us, we need to create and reward a "we're a team" attitude. For managers, we need to create and reward the management attitude — "Every employee is somebody, and every job deserves our best efforts." Finally, we need to be creative in our awards to "fit them to the person" and balance humor with serious accomplishment. We need to remember that managers in all walks of life get the credit for a lot of "behind-the-scenes" outstanding people.

THE MANTLE:

RECOGNIZING AND REWARDING GOOD PERFORMANCE

1. THE MANTLE CHURCH

a. Church leaders make an effort to say "thanks" for members' contributions of time, effort and materials.
b. Give everyone who's willing some challenging work to do for the Lord. Make every effort to use anyone who offers themselves.
c. Recognize members for accomplishing those things that have been set as personal goals in the church (e.g. an award for daily Bible reading, for evangelism, or for attending Sunday school regularly, etc.).
d. Children are rewarded for advancing to the next Sunday school class or for a Bible quiz accomplishment.
e. Because only the Lord really knows the intentions of our hearts, church leaders offer a silent recognition and reward time during some church services for a "pre-bema judgment" of our hearts by the Lord. This can be done when communion is distributed and we encourage people to "examine themselves."

2. THE MANTLE HOME

a. Parents learn to show appreciation when children do something well (planned or unplanned) in the home. There are many ways we can do this. One very meaningful way is remembering to say "Thanks" — with an extra hug or kiss for that special achievement.
b. Celebrate family member accomplishments recognized by the family's "customers." These may include school, church, employer and community (e.g. Girl

Scouts, the neighbor, Little League coach, other parents).

c. Husbands and wives recognize each other for various things like: being patient for the other partner to do something; being kind and understanding when the other partner is being stubborn and unreasonable; giving wise advice or making a smart financial decision; forgiving the other's shortcomings and failures; making the other partner look good while remaining in the background. They use many ways to "recognize" each other from flowers and balloons to more expensive gifts. One of the simplest and most meaningful ways is saying "Thanks" with hugs and kisses.

3. THE MANTLE SCHOOL

a. Teachers find special ways to reward students' achievements: besides a letter grade on a student's paper, write some comments; use a gold star or other symbol for saying, "This work is great!"; give a "pat on the back" to the student when returning his work; recognize the student before the whole class or school, when appropriate; offer the student opportunity for an advanced learning assignment.

b. Administrators find ways to recognize entire class teams—the class with the highest class average, the class with the most students being honored by the community over the past year, or the class that sold the most boosters for the football team.

c. Administrators single out teachers for special recognition at regular ceremonies — a teacher who receives her master's degree; a teacher whose students and parents have given her the highest MANTLE rating; a teacher who receives a promotion or who completed a special project to benefit the entire school; a teacher whose former students were recognized most highly by community business leaders.

Chapter Nine
RATING PERFORMANCE

*God used the **mantle**-clothed prophets to rate how people (often kings) performed. When they spoke to those being rated by God, they often reminded them of His standards. Also, they were careful to speak the whole truth and precisely cover all the things God told them to say. They did this regardless of the repercussions to themselves. **MANTLE** managers are thorough, open and honest in rating their people. They make themselves vulnerable by receiving feedback from those entrusted to them.*

Set Standards And Communicate Them To Your People

As we saw in the previous chapter, all believers in Christ shall appear before the judgment seat of Christ (2 Corinthians 5:10, Romans 14:10); and this judgment will bestow awards for what we've done while on earth. Non-believers will also have a judgment. It is the "white throne" judgment mentioned in Revelation 20:11-13:

Then I saw a great white throne and Him who sat on it, from whose face the earth and the heaven fled away. And there was found no place for them. And I saw the dead, small and great, standing before God, and books were opened. And another book was opened, which is the Book of Life. And the dead were judged according to their works, by the things which were written in the books. The sea gave up the dead who were in it, and Death and Hades delivered up the dead who were in them. And they were judged, each one according to his works.

God has set the standards by which He will rate both believers and non-believers, which He has clearly communicated through the Bible. Everyone who has a Bible has God's documented standards for living. Here are a few samples of these standards:

- "Unless one is born again, he cannot see the kingdom of God. . . . unless one is born of water and of the Spirit, he cannot enter the kingdom of God" (John 3:3,5).

- "For God so loved the world that He gave His only begotten Son, that whoever believes in Him should not perish but have everlasting life. For God did not send His Son into the world to condemn the world, but that the world through him might be saved" (John 3:16,17).

- "If you confess with your mouth the Lord Jesus and believe in your heart that God has raised Him from the dead, you shall be saved. For with the heart one believes to righteousness; and with the mouth confession is made to salvation" (Romans 10:9,10).

- "He (God) has showed you, O man, what is good; and what does the Lord require of you but to do justly, to love mercy, and to walk humbly with your God?" (Micah 6:8).

- When the Son of Man comes in His glory, and all the holy angels with Him, then He will sit upon the throne of His glory. (This is understood to be when Christ returns to earth after the Battle of Armageddon to reign on the earth as the awaited Messiah.) All the nations will be gathered before Him, and He will separate them one from another, as a shepherd divides his sheep from the goats. And He will set the sheep on his right hand, but the goats on the left. Then the King will say to those on His right hand, 'Come, you blessed of My Father, inherit the kingdom prepared for you from the foundation of the world: for I was hungry and you gave Me food; I was thirsty and you gave Me drink; I was a stranger and you took Me in; I was naked and you clothed Me; I was sick and you visited Me; I was in prison and you came to Me. . . . Inasmuch as you did it to one of the least of these My brethren, you did it to Me" (Matthew 25:31–40).

God has also set a standard for us to be His "good" and "faithful" servants (Matthew 25:21). *Good* means that we should only want what's good for others. *Faithful* means that we should trust and obey Him.

As God has set the standard and communicated what He wants from us, likewise, managers need to communicate to each employee the qualities and standards we require. We rate performance not on end results only, but also on how an employee accomplishes his work. God used the mantle-clothed prophets to rate how people (often kings) performed. When they spoke to those being rated by God, they were careful to speak precisely what God told them to say. Recall Daniel's description of God's judgment of Belshazzar, king of Babylon, "God has numbered your kingdom, and finished it. . . . You have been weighed in the balances, and found wanting. . . . Your kingdom has been divided, and given to the Medes and Persians" (Daniel 5:26-28).

As MANTLE managers, we want to provide honest feedback to our people. When we rate, because we are human beings, we have value systems that will even unconsciously influence our ratings. In organizations where rating employees is not a requirement (e.g. the church or the family), we subconsciously "rate" or "judge" performance by our value systems. These must be openly and honestly communicated to our people. Some examples are:

- Being proactive in keeping the unity of the workforce
- Sharing knowledge with others without being concerned about losing stature or position
- Diligence (e.g. dedicating themselves to a task)
- Perseverance (e.g. having a "can do, won't quit" attitude)

- Working current (e.g. lets the past be a rudder not an anchor)
- Faithfulness (e.g. can be trusted to do whatever needs to be done without the supervisor accounting for each thing and without having to be asked)
- Honesty (e.g. can be trusted to use resources as agreed)

In rating employees or in "rating" our family or church members, we should remember to "speak the truth in love" (Ephesians 4:15). As we do, remember further that as we point a finger at others, we have three fingers pointing back at ourselves. We must also be prepared to hear the truth about ourselves being spoken in love.

The Rating Interval

Another way of rating performance worth noting is similar to the way Jesus rates us. He doesn't wait until the end of our performance period (our life) to rate us. He rates us whenever we commune with Him, such as in prayer, when we feel release or conviction. He says that when we come to the altar to pray or to bring a gift to Him, if we remember that our brother has anything against us, we should leave and make things right with our brother first and then return to offer our gift (Matthew 5:23,24).

Speaking about celebrating the Lord's Supper through communion, the Apostle Paul says, "Let a man examine himself, and so let him eat of that bread and drink of that cup" (1 Corinthians 11:28). As we examine ourselves, the Lord may bring conviction of a sin that we should confess to Him so that we can be forgiven; or we may sense the peace of having no barrier of sin between us and Him. Scripture also shows us that the Lord regularly uses feedback from our brothers, sisters and teammates to admonish, encourage and correct us (Romans 15:14, Hebrews 3:13, Matthew 18:15-17).

Jesus rates us often so we can make corrections. As

74

managers we should rate our people as often as we can — not just in the formal performance appraisal process, but as feedback for how we think they're doing. We should also get our employees to "examine themselves."

We can use self appraisals along with a "profile" of feedback from peers, supervisors, subordinates and customers. We can ask our employees some key questions as part of the performance feedback process:

- What are your expectations?
- What do you think is your best accomplishment?
- What are some steps you can use to improve, and how can I help you?
- What are some accomplishments that show me your strengths?

In a world where we're being forced to downsize our work forces to produce more with less, we need to begin forming teams and rating these teams as we rate individuals. Jesus not only rates us as individuals, but also as teams.

In Revelation Chapters 2 and 3, we find a detailed description of His assessment of the seven church teams:

- The church at Ephesus was an active church, sound in doctrine, but deficient in love (2:1-7).
- The church at Smyrna was a suffering, poor church that was really rich (2:8-11).
- The church at Pergamos was heretical (2:12-17).
- The church at Thyatira was approved for its love, service and faith; but it was criticized for tolerating a false prophetess (2:18-29).
- The church at Sardis was dying (3:1-5).
- The church at Philadelphia was loyal (3:6-13).
- The church at Laodicea was lukewarm (3:14-22).

Reverse Appraisals

Most of what's been highlighted so far in this chapter has related to employees being rated by their supervisor, peers or customers; but what about a supervisor getting feedback from his employees concerning his consistency in meeting MANTLE standards? Even Jesus asked His disciples, "Who do men say that I, the Son of Man, am?" Later, He asked, "But who do you say that I am?" (Matthew 16:13-20).

We've found these "reverse appraisals" to be helpful in identifying our strengths and weaknesses. Besides our employees rating us, we managers rate ourselves against the set of questions that characterize the MANTLE model. Then, a third party gets both the manager self-rating and the employee feedback and provides a report to the manager. The next higher level manager is given his subordinate manager's report and is accountable for providing work experience and training to the subordinate manager to help him improve in the area rated weakest. We only try to build up a manager in one area at a time. The "reverse appraisal" is repeated every year to identify MANTLE behavior areas of progress and to continue picking areas for improvement. The employee ratings are kept anonymous. Each year we look at a profile of our managers as a team to determine where we need to improve as a group. By continuing this process, we've found that over time the management culture is shaped into the MANTLE model. Just as Christ is the "Omega," the ending, of the Christian life, so MANTLE is the goal for leadership behavior.

The appendix to this book provides the "reverse appraisal" forms, the feedback format given to managers, and a copy of one of our group "profiles."

THE MANTLE:
Challenges for the Church, the Home, and the School

RATING PERFORMANCE

1. THE MANTLE CHURCH

a. The Pastor, Board of Trustees, or Board of Deacons (e.g. the recognized leaders) agree upon and then make clear to all, at the beginning of the year, what is required of the Pastor and Board members for the new year. They lovingly and sincerely communicate their evaluations to each other at least semiannually.

b. Deacons (or whoever is appointed as servant leaders for church members) agree with members about specific areas for members' Christian growth (e.g. Bible study, worship, prayer, fellowship and service aspects). Loving feedback, in members' homes, is provided to them by the servant leader at least semiannually.

c. Church members encourage and accept voluntary feedback from other close church members (probably those in a small group fellowship together).

d. As a church team, we also hear from those we are serving in the community (e.g. a nursing home, senior citizens, a disabled person, a prison, missionaries, etc.) on our performance. The church team also seeks and receives an annual profile of feedback from community leaders, church members, church leaders, the pastor, and community suppliers of service to the church.

c. Church leaders encourage and get feedback on their performance from the church members and others being specifically served by that leader.

f. Time is provided for individual examinations, in the Lord's presence, as "pre-bema judgment" experiences.

2. THE MANTLE HOME

a. Each year parents discuss with children what is expected of them (e.g. jobs around the house and allowance, moral behavior, church involvement, part-time jobs, school performance and extracurricular activities. Consequences of good and bad performance are agreed upon. These are discussed with children as individuals and also as partners with brothers, sisters and parents.

b. Parents discuss performance with children at the midyear point and agree with them on how to improve performance for the rest of the year.

c. A profile on performance is provided to children with input from parents, siblings, church leaders, friends, teachers and coaches, part-time job employers and randomly selected classmates.

d. Husbands and wives discuss what they expect of each other and often lovingly express feedback to each other. Husbands, wives and parents encourage their friends, pastor or church leader, employers, and even their children to give them feedback on how they're doing.

3. THE MANTLE SCHOOL

a. At the beginning of the school year, teachers thoroughly explain to students how performance will be determined. Administrators do the same for their teachers.

b. Important behaviors that are not necessarily a formal part of the performance plan are explained to teachers by administrators and to students by teachers.

c. At the midpoint of the performance period, students and teachers are reviewed and provided explanations for improving their performance during the year.

d. Feedback to students is provided in the form of a profile with input from regular and special project teachers, test grades, peer student feedback, parent customers (e.g. a close friend's parents), coaches, and business customers (e.g. a part-time job employer).

e. Teachers and administrators are provided feedback in the form of a profile including input from students, teachers and administrators, community leader customers, the Board of Education, and parents.

Chapter Ten
DEVELOPING A HEART
FOR CUSTOMER SERVICE

As with the prophets who bore the mantle insignia, Jesus also knew well what He was called to do and whom He served. We managers need to be passionate in that knowledge as well and "cast that mantle" upon our people.

Jesus Christ's Products And Services

Jesus and His disciples have turned the world upside down and reached the heart of many millions. He did this by what we have described as MANTLE management:

- Being open to His disciples' creativity
- Being loyal and developing loyalty between Himself and His disciples
- Developing self-esteem in them
- Developing unity (and family) among them
- Communicating well and involving His disciples in planning
- Recognizing and rewarding good performance
- Rating disciples and teams well

That isn't all Jesus does to revolutionize the world. He also develops in His disciples a heart for customer service. Jesus had both product and services. As managers we need to decide with our people what we offer. The product Jesus builds is a transformed new life, free from the control of sin. He died on

Calvary's cross and shed His blood, while we were yet sinners, to pay the price for our disobedience. He rose again, the third day, so we can have newness of life in Him. Behold, all things have become new. We are a new creation after accepting Jesus Christ and His work on Calvary for us. Our sins, according to scripture, are put in the sea of forgetfulness; and God chooses to remember them no more, because Jesus' blood has covered them.

As we walk with Christ in this new life and submit to His ways instead of our ways, by our obedience to His Word, we go through the process of sanctification. This means being separated from worldly influences and being separated unto God for His work (John 17:16-19). So the product Jesus offers is a new *you* and *me*. Jesus also offers services to us. He says that He has come to minister, not to be ministered to. There are a number of services He offers:

First, He knows how hard it is to maintain our lives pure and holy, so He asks us to surrender that job to Him. He wants, as it were, for us to sign the deeds of our hearts — which have now become His home — over to Him. Then it becomes His job to maintain this new life for us, and we find that we can do all things through Christ who strengthens us. We call this service "accepting Jesus as Lord of our lives." We surrender any rights we thought we had to Him, and in return He gives us heavenly treasures as well as all we have need of on earth. More than we can ever think about or imagine becomes our inheritance.

Second, Jesus sets us into a group of believers to be built up and to contribute to building up others. He offers us His service of making us servants of one another. He does this to give us real life and worth and to give it more abundantly! As Jesus washed the feet of His disciples, He offers us that ministry too. So we who are Christians become servants to one another giving us "meat" to eat that most unbelievers can't comprehend. It's the meat of doing God's will for other believers. We find that we are in a battle together — living this Christian life — and we need one another. We are dependent upon God and each other. The life is not just "Jesus and me" but a life lived out in a corporate body, where the objective is to glorify God and become one with brothers and sisters in the Christian family (Acts 2:42-47). Fellow Christians become internal customers of one another receiving Jesus' provision through other believers.

Third, Jesus empowers believers to witness to the world — those who have not yet accepted Jesus' product or services, by giving them the Baptism of the Holy Spirit. John the Baptist spoke about this service when he said of Jesus, "I indeed baptize you with water, but . . . He will baptize you with the Holy Spirit and with fire" (Luke 3:16). Jesus told His disciples to wait in Jerusalem, after He ascended into heaven, "until you are endued with power from on high" (Luke 24:49). "Wait for the promise of the Father, which, He said, you have heard from Me. For John truly baptized with water; but you shall be baptized with the Holy Spirit not many days from now. But you shall receive power when the Holy Spirit has come upon you; and you shall be witnesses to Me in Jerusalem, and in all Judea and Samaria, and to the end of the earth" (Acts 1:4,5,8). In other words, Jesus empowers believers to go make more disciples. Thus, unbelievers become external customers who need to be informed about the product and services Jesus is providing.

Finally, Jesus develops in His believers a heart for satisfying His primary customer, His Heavenly Father. He does this by His example — His actions and His words.

Everyone has a customer, internal or external to the organization. Managers and employees need to identify who their real customers are and work toward delighting them. Your customer is the one who receives your product or service and who can make or break your enterprise. In profit-making companies, it's the one who most affects the bottom line. For Jesus, that customer was His Heavenly Father, who sent Him. His product, a new *you* and *me*, is made so that we can have a right relationship with the Father. It was born in the heart of the

Father from the foundation of the world to send His Son to free mankind from the control of sin. It was also the Father to whom Jesus needed to present Himself, after His resurrection from the dead, to have the Father certify that what He had done satisfied that cause (John 20:17). Again it was His Father who said, "This is My beloved Son, in whom I am well pleased" (Matthew 3:17; 17:5).

Even as a boy, Jesus knew who He needed to satisfy. In a visit to Jerusalem with His earthly parents, He separated Himself from them. They found Him in the temple speaking to the religious leaders of the day. When they inquired what He was doing, Jesus replied, "Why is it that you sought Me? Did you not know that I must be about My Father's business?" (Luke 2:49). It was being about His Father's business that characterized Jesus' life and ministry. Jesus taught us by example how to submit to the Father's will: "Most assuredly, I say to you, the Son can do nothing of Himself, but what He sees the Father do; for whatever He does, the Son does in like manner" (John 5:19). "He who does not honor the Son also does not honor the Father who sent Him" (John 5:23). "My Father is greater than I" (John 14:28).

Jesus spoke of two places that needed to be prepared — one by Him and one by us in John 14:2,23. The first was, "In My Father's house are many mansions . . . I go to prepare a place for you." The second was, "If anyone loves Me, he will keep My words; and My Father will love him, and We will come to him and make Our home with him."

In both cases, note the way Jesus lifts up His Father — His prime customer. Remember the many times Jesus left His disciples to go to a private place to pray to His Heavenly Father — perhaps to check how He was satisfying the Father. Remember also Jesus' prayer at Gethsemane, "Father, if it is Your will, remove this cup from Me; nevertheless not My will, but Yours, be done" (Luke 22:42).

It wasn't the spikes that held Jesus to the cross. It was His love for sinners and His desire to please His Father in every "moment of truth."

Moments Of Truth

We managers need to develop the same heart for customer service in workers as Jesus does in His disciples. We must teach them to effectively manage every "moment of truth" — every opportunity that the customer has to evaluate the service to them.

To illustrate this idea of moments of truth, consider a customer who enters a restaurant. The first opportunity for the customer to evaluate the service might be the cleanliness or ambiance he senses. The next "moment" might be if he is greeted warmly. Next, the customer might evaluate the service by how the menu is presented to him and whether he is advised of the specials for the day. There is one moment of truth that restaurants are especially sensitive to. It's when two guests, at the same table, order the exact same meal, such as t-bone steaks. When their meals are served, restaurants have found that the next "moment" is when customers look at each other's plate to see if the other person got a larger portion. Whoever gets the smaller serving never returns to the restaurant. Now, many restaurants carefully weigh the steaks before cooking and serving them.

Jesus experienced many such moments:

- When the Pharisees tried to trap Him into saying or doing things against the Law or against Caesar
- When the woman was caught in adultery, and He said, "He who is without sin among you, let him throw a stone at her first" (John 8:7)
- When He was in the Pharisee Simon's house and the woman who was known by all to be a sinner came in and washed His feet with her tears and wiped them with her hair — and when Simon questioned Him about it He said, in essence, that whoever He forgives the most, loves Him the most" (Luke 7:36-50)

Oh how delighted His customer, His Heavenly Father, must have been with Jesus' management of those moments of truth; and of course, He was delighted when His Son willingly suffered for all those who would accept Him and His work on Calvary to be freed from the penalty of eternal separation from the Father. Oh, how happy we — Jesus' other customers — are that He gave His life for ours.

How To Develop A Passion For Customer Service

Every enterprise has its products, services, managers, employees and customers. Managers need to build roads and bridges to their workers by being MANTLE managers — motivating them by using a participative and spirit-building management philosophy. We also need to go one very important step further and give them a heart for customer service. For our enterprise to be truly all it can be, we need to develop a passion in our people to serve the customer. Some have said that *knowledge* is the most important element in preparing our people for service, but I believe that passion is at least as important. If a worker doesn't have the knowledge he needs but has a sincere desire to please the customer, he will acquire the knowledge (time permitting) or will get someone who has the knowledge to help make that moment with the customer successful.

Whatever the enterprise, we need to develop in our people the idea of customers — and with this customer concept, we need to develop the idea of moments of truth.

Managers need to be creative in instilling these ideas into their people. We need to be like the Disney Corporation, which teaches its employees at Disney World that they are entertainers for the customer — whether they sweep the streets of Fantasy Land or dress as Mickey Mouse. They don't wear "uniforms." They wear "costumes." Everyone is an entertainer who's there to make the customer feel good about his visit. We need to give employees at least as much concern for delighting the customer as their supervisors have.

What about non-profit organizations? Who are their customers? Take the family as an example. A family's product could be the children who are raised to be loving, responsible and productive adults. That product could be love and unity between husband and wife that demonstrate to friends, extended family, and a watching world how love is patient and kind; how it doesn't envy or get puffed up with pride; how it's courteous and honest and isn't easily provoked; how love bears, believes, hopes and endures all things (1 Corinthians 13:4-7). Customers of such a family could be:

- The Lord, who gets worshipped and loved
- The community that gets the benefit of a doctor, mechanic, counselor or other services generated
- The extended family, such as grandparents, who get to be loved and to love this family
- Employers who get the productivity and talents developed in the family
- Schools that get the obedience, cooperation and team spirit given by the products of the family
- The church that benefits from the spiritual values manifested and the Sunday school, children's church, or other volunteer services given by the family

Building a heart for customer service starts with the manager showing his personal concern for providing the best possible product or service. This can't just be verbal assent, but must be one that is visible and persistent. Husbands can begin by recognizing and nurturing their wives' special gifts and abilities that apply to serving others. Parents and teachers can do the same for their children and students. Wives can gently nudge their husbands to make those phone calls or social visits that they're reluctant to make. Also, both husbands and wives can sacrifice time with each other that can be used in the service of others.

Some ideas that have worked for me in the workplace may

be helpful. We decided that we needed something to measure our success. One very important measurement was to receive high scores from customers. We developed customer survey cards that are given out with each product or service delivered. We've found that allowing employees to sign their names on the cards helps them know that their supervisors are really interested in feeding back to them, as individuals, what the customer says about their work. We let that card come right back to the worker so he sees exactly what was said about his work. If the work was unsatisfactory, we involve the employee and his supervisor in finding out from the customer what was wrong and how the product could have been better. On a monthly basis, we post charts so both customers and employees can see how the customers assessed the unit's work, from the cards that were returned. Trend charts are developed showing results over longer periods of time, such as quarterly or yearly, to determine consistency of quality and timeliness. These trends are presented at quarterly manager conferences where managers discuss what can be done to improve customer service and product quality.

Other ways we use to build this "heart" for customers are to present letters of appreciation from customers at the quarterly award ceremony and mention these at times in our newsletter to employees. Having customers tour our facilities and having our workers visit the customers' sites to see how they use the product or service is something we are considering to increase customer sensitivity. Our customers are members of the same government agency as we are. Whether customers are internal to your organization or external, the result will be developing a passion for customer support. We are now pioneering the implementation of two self-directed work teams for which customer ratings will influence individual performance ratings. Since this is being introduced after years of customer surveys, chart posting, and trend development, it's easier for our employees to accept customers influencing their ratings.

Serving the customer well yourself and setting the example

for your people carries a lot of weight with your employees' development. This is especially true when they see you deal with an unreasonable customer by demonstrating the attitude: "The customer may not always be right, but he is always the customer!" Remember, it wasn't the nails that held Jesus to the cross!

Using this customer service perspective and agreeing upon customers, products and services help MANTLE managers and our people focus more clearly on what it means to be "successful" in our enterprises. They allow us to identify the real "measures" of success. They also help us involve our people in setting a few specific, easy-to-understand, clearly-visible goals and objectives so we can "kick" hardest — like runners in a race — as we see the finish line in view.

THE MANTLE:
Challenges for the Church, the Home, and the School

DEVELOPING A HEART FOR SATISFYING THOSE WE SERVE (E.G. OUR "CUSTOMERS")

1. THE MANTLE CHURCH

a. Pastors and church leaders discuss and agree on who are those that the church serves.
b. Establish, communicate to, and equip church members concerning who the church really serves. First, we serve the Lord. Second, we serve one another and those who may become Christians through our cooperation with the Lord in (1) our homes, workplaces and neighborhoods; (2) our towns; (3) surrounding communities. Deacons have people assigned to them to call and lovingly coach about Bible study, fellowship, worship, prayer, and service in their Christian lives.
c. Establish, communicate to, and equip church members concerning the church's expected "fruits" including (1) born-again Christians shaped into

87

the image of Christ; (2) homeless, sick, imprisoned people who are ministered to by church members; (3) men, women, boys and girls who are encouraged to receive Christ and are helped as they live the Christian life.

d. Establish, communicate, set and monitor goals for measuring success. What will the Lord use at the bema judgment to measure us individually or measure the local church team? (1) *A measure of Christian maturity*. Sunday school attendance; Bible study attendance; church ministry participation; number of young people attending Bible Colleges; percent of members involved in serving in the church; (2) *A measure of evangelism efforts*. Number of witnessing opportunities; number of born-again experiences inside or outside the church; (3) *A measure of being our "brother's keeper."* Number of food or clothing packages to the homeless; visitations to the sick or imprisoned; opportunities for ministering to the community senior citizens, nursing homes, and hospitals; number of regular small home fellowship groups; (4) *A measure of our devotion to the Lord*. Number of members involved in worship opportunities provided by the church; number of members who tithe; number of members involved in daily personal Bible study and prayer.

e. The church celebrates successes.

2. THE MANTLE HOME

a. Parents, children, husbands and wives discuss and agree upon who the family serves. The family primarily serves the Lord, who is worshipped and loved. The family also serves as its members provide skilled professional and nonprofessional services to the community. The extended family members are served too because they get to love and be loved by this family. Employers are served. Schools and churches also receive services from family members.

88

b. Once we establish who is served, the family equips itself to serve these "customers." This is done by arranging our schedules to allow sufficient time to actively participate and arranging our finances to support those whom we've decided to serve. It requires our using the best sources of training and information (e.g. family Bible study and prayer).

c. The family identifies what results they want to achieve. For example, a family with or without children may decide that producing a genuine love between family members is their greatest product. Another family could decide that producing loving, responsible and productive adults out of their children is their greatest product. Another could decide that helping one another achieve their individual goals (e.g. being a doctor) would be their best service. In most cases, it's probably some combination of these.

d. The family decides how to measure success and communicates this to its members: (1) good feedback from the school, the church, the workplace, the community; (2) demonstrations of sincere affection between family members; (3) making grandparents happy; (4) graduating college; (5) children begin at an early age earning their own money.

e. The family celebrates successes.

3. THE MANTLE SCHOOL

a. Teachers and students discuss who the class serves. Administrators and teachers discuss who the school serves. A class may decide they serve the school (e.g. the class of 1994 leaves a legacy of achievements and good examples for the class of 1995). The faculty may decide they serve the community (e.g. local businesses and other employers, the Town Council), the home, the Board of Education, the next higher school (e.g. the secondary school or colleges and universities).

b. Once it's decided *who* the class or school serves, it equips itself to serve them. Curriculum, books, special projects, guest lecturers, field trips, the school budget, parent-teacher sessions, faculty-business leader sessions, etc. are oriented around *who* is being served.

c. Teachers and students, administrators and teachers decide what results they want to achieve. They may decide to build students who are the best they can be scholastically, socially and morally, who are civic-minded, creative, responsible and accountable for their actions. They understand the reality of getting good paying jobs but also feel a sense of duty to offer themselves voluntarily where needed to serve. They are outstanding individually and also as teammates.

d. Administrators, teachers and students decide how to measure success: (1) good feedback from the community, the home, the Board of Education, and the next higher school system being served; (2) the grades achieved on college board examinations or other State or National achievement tests; (3) degree of participation in school social and sports functions; (4) decreases in immoral, corrupt or abusive behavior; (5) degree of volunteerism demonstrated by students; (6) percent of students attending and finishing college; (7) feedback from peers on fellow student cooperation on team projects.

e. The school celebrates successes.

Chapter Eleven
THE SAME YESTERDAY, TODAY AND FOREVER

Management We Can (And Will) Emulate

Have you heard the story of the little girl who once said to her mother, "I like you better than God"? The mother quickly replied, "Oh, you must not say that"; but the child insisted until her mother finally said, "Sweety, what makes you say that?" The little girl answered simply, "Because I can hug you!"

That child expressed in her innocent way the universal desire of mankind to have contact with God in a personal, tangible way. A spirit is hard for us to conceive, but a real "flesh and bones" man is a concrete reality we can understand. That's exactly what Jesus did for us in the incarnation. He brought God within "hugging" distance. Not only could man see, hear and feel Him; but we could also emulate Him. This book was written to help us emulate His example of MANTLE management. We've also used the mantle garment to illustrate attributes of Jesus' leadership behaviors.

The Apostle Peter knew that people deserved to be listened to and treated with dignity. He knew that Jesus' management was strong but sensitive and serving, gentle and respectful, open and honest, empowering and trusting. He knew that it included the authority of a consistent example. Peter wrote to the early church leaders, "Be shepherds of God's flock that is under your care, serving as overseers — not because you must, but because you are willing, as God wants you to be; not greedy for money, but eager to serve; not lording it over those entrusted to you, but being examples to the flock" (1 Peter 5:2-3 NIV).

To assess the future value of MANTLE management, consider the following: The prophet Zechariah told of the Branch, "From His place He shall branch out, and He shall build the temple of the Lord . . . He shall bear the glory, and shall sit and rule on His throne; so He shall be a priest on His throne" (Zechariah 6:12,13).

For believers, this speaks of the return of Jesus to rule the world from Jerusalem. Note it speaks of Him not only as being King, but also as being a Priest (or one who serves the people). In the Book of Revelation, we also have references to Jesus making His disciples "kings and priests to His God and Father" (Revelation 1:6). "And have made us kings and priests to our God; and we shall reign on the earth" (Revelation 5:10). So not only will Jesus be both King and Priest, but believers will also return with Him and be made "kings and priests."

Believers will be ruler-priests, who will have leadership authority, while at the same time be commissioned to serve the people they are ruling. Jesus is the same yesterday, today, and *forever* (Hebrews 13:8). His management concepts, which He has already given us to understand and embrace, will be those that He will follow Himself and that He will want us to emulate when He returns to rule the earth.

We need to turn the pyramid upside down and begin thinking of the front line people — those who actually "touch" the customers — as being most important for the success of our enterprise. We need to build them up and empower them so that within prescribed, agreed-upon boundaries of authority, they can speak and act on our behalf and feel our concerns for the business, church, family or school.

We must equip them with problem-solving techniques, both as individuals and as teams. We need to provide the motivation by communicating well — by incorporating their thinking into our planning, and by providing open and honest rating systems with rewards for good performance. We also need to develop in them a heart for customers by our own example and by establishing measurements of success.

"King-priest" MANTLE management excellence may be difficult to attain and require our utmost attention and energy. It will certainly go against our human nature. Its value may not be recognized at first — just as Christ was not recognized by the religious leaders of His day. The downward spiral, however, of our vital enterprises, speaks loudly that we most certainly must continuously strive to improve the quality of our management performance. The other "mantles" being worn by leaders are frayed and unraveling. What greater goal is there for a workplace manager, pastor, deacon, teacher, parent, coach, *leader* than to follow in the path of the Master Manager, King of kings and Lord of lords, who is also the Lamb upon the Throne (Revelation 17:14; 22:1,3)?

Accept the king-priest mantle and dress for success in leading your enterprise!

APPENDIX

Management Thru Leadership (MANTLE) Survey

Employee's Perception of Leadership

ORG. NAME	DATE	MGR/TEAM LDR NAME

PLEASE CIRCLE CHOICE

QUESTIONS	Unable To Meet This Mantle Standard Consistently					Able To Meet This Mantle Standard Consistently
	LOWEST						HIGHEST
1. Being open to new ideas and opinions of workers.	1	2	3	4	5	6	7
2. Encourages workers' input to what the goals should be.	1	2	3	4	5	6	7
3. Allows workers to control their own work life with very little interference from mgr except for when problems occur.	1	2	3	4	5	6	7
4. Being a good listener to worker problems.	1	2	3	4	5	6	7
5. Trusts the workers to resolve problems and not take over.	1	2	3	4	5	6	7
6. Treats people as individuals rather than all the same, especially in attempting to resolve problems.	1	2	3	4	5	6	7
7. Allows employees liberal training in job related areas, if money is available.	1	2	3	4	5	6	7
8. Motivates employees by using a mix of various awards and gives them verbal praise.	1	2	3	4	5	6	7
9. Fosters innovation in workers (i.e., encourages creativity).	1	2	3	4	5	6	7
10. Creates a Team Spirit environment among workers.	1	2	3	4	5	6	7
11. Keeps employees informed by using staff meeting/town meetings and informal/formal modes of communications.	1	2	3	4	5	6	7
12. Rates workers on performance by explaining very openly how they will be rated (i.e., tells them what qualities they look for that are not in the GPAS standard (i.e., cooperation, etc.)).	1	2	3	4	5	6	7
13. Develops a commitment in employees for providing good customer service.	1	2	3	4	5	6	7
14. To what degree does this manager add value to the organization.	1	2	3	4	5	6	7

If you have any other suggestions or complaints about any aspect of service provided, please use this space.

FEEDBACK FROM EMPLOYEES' EVALUATION
USING THE MANagement Thru LEadership
(MANTLE) MODEL

THE MANTLE 14-POINTS RATED BY EMPLOYEES FOR:
SUPERVISOR Y (THE RATING BELOW IS LISTED BY STRONGEST
AREA - TO - WEAKEST AREA.)

6.1 (14)	The degree of value added by this manager.
5.9 (3)	Allows workers to control their own work life with very little interference from mgr except for when problems occur.
5.9 (13)	Develops a heart in employees for providing good customer service.
5.8 (4)	Being a good listener to a workers' problems.
5.8 (11)	Keeps employees informed by using staff meetings, town meetings, and informal/formal modes of communications.
5.8 (9)	Fosters innovation in workers (e.g., encourages creativity).
5.7 (1)	Being open to new ideas and opinions of workers.
5.7 (8)	Motivates employees by using a mix of various awards and gives them verbal praise.
5.7 (6)	Treats people as individuals rather than all the same, especially in attempting to resolve problems.
5.7 (2)	Encourages workers' input to what the goals should be.
5.7 (10)	Creates a Team Spirit environment among workers.
5.6 (5)	Trusts the workers to resolve problems and not "take over."
5.5 (7)	Allows employees liberal training in job related areas, if money is available.
5.5 (12)	Rates workers on performance by explaining very openly how they will be rated (e.g., telling them what qualities the supervisor values (e.g., cooperation, etc.)).

AVERAGE OF ALL RATINGS - 5.7
HIGHEST RATING = 6.1 LOWEST RATING = 5.3

MANAGER'S SELF-RATING FURTHEST ABOVE
THE EMPLOYEES' RATING #2
(Gap = manager's self rating - the employees' rating - 1.3)

MANAGER'S SELF-RATING FARTHEST BELOW
THE EMPLOYEES' RATING #7
(Gap = employees' rating - the manager's self-rating - 2.5)

MANTLE OUTLYER SCORES

These scores represent the total number of employee's that rated a manager two points "above" or two points "below" the overall average score on each question, based on the rating scale 1 - 7.

QUESTIONS	ABOVE	BELOW
1	2	0
2	1	0
3	0	0
4	1	0
5	1	0

MANTLE PROFILE
AVERAGE RATING ON EACH QUESTION

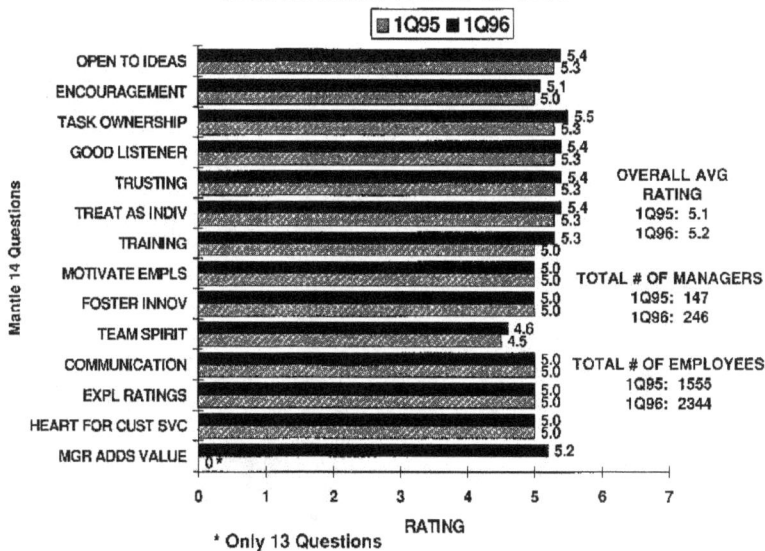

Legend: 1Q95 ■ 1Q96

Mantle 14 Questions	1Q95	1Q96
OPEN TO IDEAS	5.4	5.3
ENCOURAGEMENT	5.1	5.0
TASK OWNERSHIP	5.5	5.3
GOOD LISTENER	5.4	5.3
TRUSTING	5.4	5.3
TREAT AS INDIV	5.4	5.3
TRAINING	5.3	5.0
MOTIVATE EMPLS	5.0	5.0
FOSTER INNOV	5.0	5.0
TEAM SPIRIT	4.6	4.5
COMMUNICATION	5.0	5.0
EXPL RATINGS	5.0	5.0
HEART FOR CUST SVC	5.0	5.0
MGR ADDS VALUE	0*	5.2

RATING (scale 0 to 7)

* Only 13 Questions

OVERALL AVG RATING
1Q95: 5.1
1Q96: 5.2

TOTAL # OF MANAGERS
1Q95: 147
1Q96: 246

TOTAL # OF EMPLOYEES
1Q95: 1555
1Q96: 2344

COMPARISON - PROFILE - MANTLE
FOR SUPERVISOR X

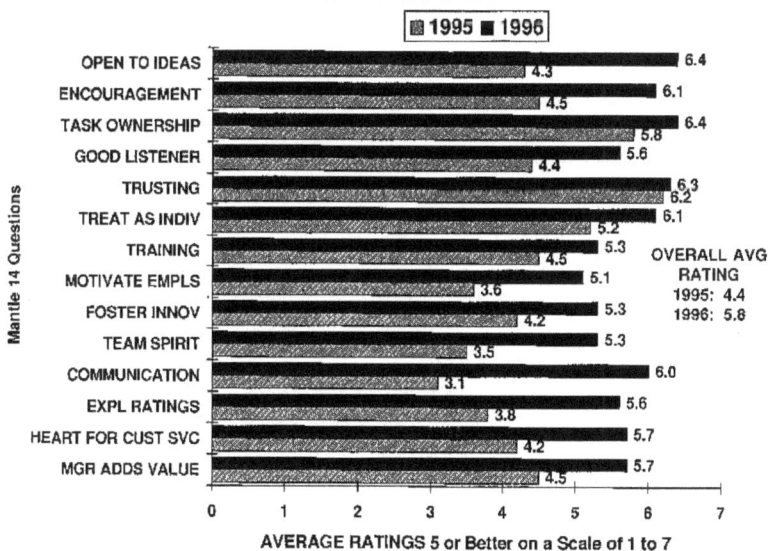

Legend: 1995 ■ 1996

Mantle 14 Questions	1995	1996
OPEN TO IDEAS	4.3	6.4
ENCOURAGEMENT	4.5	6.1
TASK OWNERSHIP	5.8	6.4
GOOD LISTENER	4.4	5.6
TRUSTING	6.2	6.3
TREAT AS INDIV	5.2	6.1
TRAINING	4.5	5.3
MOTIVATE EMPLS	3.6	5.1
FOSTER INNOV	4.2	5.3
TEAM SPIRIT	3.5	5.3
COMMUNICATION	3.1	6.0
EXPL RATINGS	3.8	5.6
HEART FOR CUST SVC	4.2	5.7
MGR ADDS VALUE	4.5	5.7

AVERAGE RATINGS 5 or Better on a Scale of 1 to 7

OVERALL AVG RATING
1995: 4.4
1996: 5.8

INDEX

To order more copies of *The Mantle: How to Dress for Success in Leadership* or to receive a catalog of other books published by Mantle Ministries, write:

MANTLE MINISTRIES
PO BOX 248
Lanoka Harbor, NJ 08734

Please send me _____ copies of *The Mantle:How to Dress for Success in Leadership* by James Biscardi @ $9.95 per copy.

Name _____

Address _____

City _____ State _____ Zip _____

Please send this coupon, check or money order to:

MANTLE MINISTRIES
PO BOX 248
Lanoka Harbor, NJ 08734

* Make checks payable to Mantle Ministries.

Shipping/Handling		Subtotal $_____
Order		Total $_____
Up to $10	$2	
$10 - $25	$4	
$25 & up	FREE	

Thank you for your order. God bless you!

Managers
Must Trust...
Confidence in
Their People!

As the mantle protected the prophet, Christlike leaders help their people withstand the storms of life. "Stand fast in one spirit, with one mind striving together for the faith of the gospel." Philippians 1:27.

What Readers Say...

"What a delightful book...very well done and based solidly upon scriptural principles. I will use some material for seminar work." – Reverend Charles Crabtree, Assistant Superintendent Assemblies of God, Springfield, Missouri.

"The Mantle is an excellent help for Christians who are leaders and managers in the 'real world'. And for my pastor and me, it's proven to be an excellent study for retreats." – Bob Wishon, Metro Director Christian Business Men's Committee, Fanwood, New Jersey.

"Through the imagery of Elijah's mantle, Jim Biscardi paints a vivid picture of Jesus' servant leadership. Readers discover that the duality of leading by serving nurtures relationships, and actually becomes the catalyst for mutuality and personal growth. Reading The Mantle revitalizes Jesus' vision for us as co-servants and co-leaders with Him." – Dawn Sharp, New Jersey Christian Ministries, Inc., Piscataway, New Jersey.

"I'm reading this book for the third time so that I can receive from the Lord all of its richness." – Pastor Selwyn Sills, Abundant Life Assembly of God Church, Linden, Guyana, South America

"In an age where true leadership is in short supply, it is essential that we find and foster models that return us to the

What Readers Say...Continued

heart of what makes a leader. As a pastor, I and my congregation have greatly benefited from the model Jim Biscardi presents. With a firm hold on the Word of God and a critical eye on today's world, The Mantle, offers a clear and practical handle on the issue of servant-leadership." – Reverend Scott Nichols, Pastor Faith Reformed Church, Midland Park, New Jersey.

"Very refreshing. It helped me clean and press my own mantle." – Reverend Ralph M. Thomas, Center for Hope Hospice, Linden, New Jersey.

"The Mantle is a good reference book to read and re-read. It gives God's principles for making our business successful while at the same time we fulfill God's will in caring for people." – Mrs. Carol Fasseas, Homeaker and Businesswoman, Livingston, New Jersey.

"This book has given me a new and different perspective on what should be the appropriate behavior for a Christian in a work, family, church, and education environment. Whatever 'mantle of authority' one wears on his exterior as a manager/leader, the more difficult mantle is the one on his interior as a Christian in an 'upside-down pyramid' – a showpiece to follow in the path of the Master Manager, Jesus Christ." – Professor C.N. Woerner, Adj. Professor, Business Management, Union County College, Union, New Jersey.